Joseph Joubert

Joubert -- Some of the Toughts

Joseph Joubert

Joubert -- Some of the Toughts

ISBN/EAN: 9783337732820

Printed in Europe, USA, Canada, Australia, Japan

Cover: Foto ©ninafisch / pixelio.de

More available books at **www.hansebooks.com**

JOUBERT.

Charles Eliot Norton, editor of the *North American Review*, has been lecturing before the Parker Fraternity, Boston. He was very curt in his reference to this city. We quote: "Our rich men do not know how to use their wealth, and there is no country where the wealthy get so poor a return for their riches as in this country. Mr. Astor has given a few hundred thousand dollars to found a library for which a million would have been too little. Mr. Cooper has established an Institute with a good endowment, but the plan upon which it is established makes it almost worthless. Mr. Cornell has founded a University, which will be an honor to his State, but he does not belong to New York city. In all that marks true culture, New York is lamentably deficient, and it is rare indeed to find a man in New York city who gives much time to thinking."

HIST. DE FRANCE.

JOUBERT.

JOUBERT.

SOME OF THE "THOUGHTS" OF JOSEPH JOUBERT.

TRANSLATED BY

GEORGE H. CALVERT,
AUTHOR OF "FIRST YEARS IN EUROPE," "THE GENTLEMAN," ETC.

PRECEDED BY A NOTICE OF JOUBERT

BY THE TRANSLATOR.

BOSTON:
WILLIAM V. SPENCER.
1867.

Entered according to Act of Congress, in the year 1866, by
GEORGE H. CALVERT,
In the Clerk's Office of the District Court for the District of Rhode Island.

CAMBRIDGE:
STEREOTYPED BY H. O. HOUGHTON AND COMPANY.

Presswork by John Wilson and Sons.

CONTENTS.

	PAGE
NOTICE OF JOSEPH JOUBERT	vii
I. OF GOD, CREATION, ETERNITY, PIETY, RELIGION	31
II. THE CHAPTERS. (LES CHAPITRES)	40
III. OF MAN, OF ORGANS, THE SOUL AND THE INTELLECTUAL FACULTIES	46
IV. OF THE NATURE OF MINDS	51
V. OF THE PASSIONS AND THE AFFECTIONS OF THE SOUL	58
VI. WHAT IS MODESTY?	66
VII. OF THE DIFFERENT AGES, OF LIFE, DISEASE, AND DEATH	74
VIII. OF THE FAMILY AND OF HOME, OF SOCIETY, CONVERSATION, POLITENESS, AND MANNERS	80
IX. OF WISDOM, VIRTUE, MORALITY, RULE, AND DUTY	86
X. OF ORDER AND CHANCE, OF GOOD AND EVIL, OF TRUTH AND ERROR	91
XI. OF PHILOSOPHY, OF METAPHYSIC, OF ABSTRACTIONS, OF LOGIC, OF SYSTEMS; OF SPACE, OF TIME, OF LIGHT, OF AIR, ETC.	97
XII. OF GOVERNMENTS AND CONSTITUTIONS; OF LIBERTY, OF JUSTICE AND THE LAWS; OF PUBLIC AND PRIVATE MORALS, OF THE CHARACTER OF NATIONS	104
XIII. OF ANTIQUITY; OF THE AGE	115

		PAGE
XIV.	OF EDUCATION; OF THE FINE ARTS; OF POETRY; OF STYLE	122
XV.	OF THE QUALITIES OF THE WRITER, AND OF LITERARY COMPOSITION	135
XVI.	LITERARY JUDGMENTS	152

NOTICE OF JOSEPH JOUBERT.

L<i>E vrai, le beau, le juste, le saint :</i> " The true, the beautiful, the just, the holy." These were the last words written by Joubert, words which sum the aims and prepossessions of his life. Who was Joseph Joubert ? A native of France, born in 1754, in a small town of Perigord, who entered manhood at the College of Toulouse, half pupil, half teacher, and beloved as both. Impelled by early devotion to letters, Joubert went, in 1778, to Paris ; knew Marmontel, Laharpe, d'Alembert ; was intimate with the prince of French talkers of that restless sparkling era, Diderot ; passed unscathed through the ordeal of French philosophism ; in 1790 was chosen, though long absent, chief magistrate of his native town of Montignac ; retired 1792 to Villeneuve in Burgundy, to be married and to pursue his studies and meditations ; survived the *Reign of Terror;* thenceforward passed his life between Villeneuve and Paris, the friend of Madame de Beaumont, of Fontanes, Chateaubriand, Molé; in 1809 was appointed one of the Regents of the University, and died in 1824. Such were the successive epochs in the quiet career of Joubert.

M. Paul de Raynal, his biographer and editor, says of him, that he was " ever more bent on bettering himself than on making himself talked of; more desirous of perfection than of fame." This is the key to the mind of Joubert; and the golden key opens a chamber of treasures. Dedicated to letters, this pure aspiring quality makes him a very type of the literary spirit, which, in its genuineness, ever prompts to the attainment of the best for its own sake. " The beautiful," he says, " is beauty seen with the eyes of the soul;" pursuing and enlarging the thought, he might have added, that beauty is the world seen with the eyes of the soul; for man and all things on earth, beheld with this transfiguring vision, are so lapt and fused in light, that, like the commonest fibre or atom looked at through a microscope, they one and all glow into bloom and symmetry. Of this soaring characteristic of Joubert, one of his French commentators, M. Eugene Poitou, thus speaks: " The trait which first strikes one in Joubert is a natural elevation: it is as though an inward force lifted him from the earth, as though his soul were ever mindful of heaven, and, an exile and captive here, ceaselessly tended to remount to its first home."

The ethic and the æsthetic do not imply one the other. Men of purest sentiment and practice may have a weak sense of the beautiful; and poetic power is sometimes divorced from moral. In Joubert they were intermarried. " In literary work let there be no separation between the intellect and the soul," was one of his heartfelt maxims; and being drawn by his nature to look at things from their poetic side, in this double illumination he saw them with a rare clearness and judged of them through an insight that gave to many of his sentences the truth and vividness of revelations: his pages are filled with light.

To Joubert's apartment in the *rue St. Honoré*, at the top of a tall house, — that he might, as he playfully said, have as much of heaven and as little of earth as possible, — came many of the choice spirits of Paris, drawn thither by the charm of the man and the thinker, — a charm resulting from the union of soul with subtlety, of amenity with intellectuality, of a genial, sympathetic personal bearing with deep plentiful resources. And so strong was this attractiveness, that often when he was ill in bed (his health was never strong) Madame Joubert had to stand guard at his chamber door, to keep out visitors, eager for the disclosures of his tongue. He was, in fact, a high teacher, teaching the cultivated, the thoughtful, the aspiring, with his talk ; for, though often urged to it by his lettered friends, he published no book. Happily, from his twentieth year to his seventieth, he jotted down with pencil, the best issues of his meditation as they arose ; and out of this chaos of notes was shaped, many years after his death, a full volume of " Thoughts," which, from their freshness and insight, their concise symmetry of expression, their pithiness, their variety, make a rich enduring addition to the literature of France, and to all literature. His critical thoughts have mostly more fineness and delicacy, and more precision and less worldliness than those of La Bruyère. His thoughts on God, on religion, on man, on duty, are less austere and formal than those of Pascal, more tolerant, with a warmer humanity in them, and a cheerfulness which comes chiefly from superior spirituality, and he has a freer imaginative play. As Joubert had, moreover, the benefit of the richer modern influences, and of the discipline of the great French Revolution, he may be called a Pascal and La Bruyère, with a fuller, finer culture than either, and a more spiritual illumination.

A thoughtful, religious, æsthetic nature, Joubert's meditations rounded themselves into compact sentences on all the great themes of human thought and experience ; and, from his early manhood to his latest years, taking especial joy in literature, and the quality of his mind being imaginative as well as spiritual, his standard was very high, and hence the fruits of his meditation the more choice and unspotted. He declares, that " nothing is more beautiful than a beautiful book." To create such a one, the soul, he believed, must be blest with a gentle perpetual enthusiasm, a latent sublime ardor ; and this permanent blessing was on himself.

From every page of the literary chapters passages might be cited to illustrate the originality, the soundness, the perspicacity, the elevation of Joubert's literary opinions and his felicity of expression. I take two or three for exemplification and comment. Towards the end of a short section entitled, *On some romances of the day*, aimed at French " sensation novels " of fifty years ago. a principle is enunciated which — could it be honored as a critical canon — would save much more than a vast present waste of ink and paper. " When fiction is not more beautiful than reality it has no right to be. . . In literature the object of Art is the beautiful. If Art falls into the domain of bald reality, it goes beyond its limits and is lost." And who has the gift to meet the demand of Joubert, and make fiction more beautiful than reality, so enriching the personages of the pen with ideal blood that they shall step forth wreathed with beauty and enduring life ? Only some Sterne, or Goethe, or Cervantes, or Shakespeare. To vitalize fiction there is needed creative faculty, with rare parts to work with. Thence, novels as a class are shallow and lifeless. To write them (except the very best) denotes æsthetic defect, want of a lively exacting sense of beauty ; for, to give one's self wholly to such work implies what is incompatible with the activity of this sense, namely, the steeping of the mind in silent mental excitement, through the rapid presentation to the fancy of passional conjunctions, the multiplication of prosaic details, and the exaggeration of situations. In writers of them, and in readers of them, novels wear the sensibilities and impair the taste, in that they have neither deeps nor tranquillity, and neither invite to, nor would bear, quiet contemplation, being in this the opposite of nature and of pure Art. Even the better kinds hurry you through their chapters by sudden shocks and impulsions, and are neither real nor ideal enough to have depths. By stretching the faculties in pursuit of shadows, by pawning the feelings on phantoms, they waste the virility of the mind. On the other hand, high fiction, that which is poetically imaginative, is bracing, elevating, refining. The best literature tranquilizes while it animates and strengthens the reader, and has in it something " heaven-y-pointing."

Most of Joubert's literary judgments are, like the one just quoted, broad truths, practical truths, reached by fineness and sureness of perception, which were the result of a rare instinct cultivated and chastened by long intellectual and moral discipline ; as, for example, what he says, in a letter to M. Molé, of force in writing: "Mere force is not power: some authors have more muscle than talent. Force is a quality which is only then praiseworthy when it is either concealed or clothed. In the ordinary sense Lucan had more than Plato, Brébeuf than Racine." And, it may be added, Carlyle more than Coleridge, Richter more than Goethe. Goethe broadly exemplifies the position of Joubert. In no author is there more inward power with so little outward exhibition. In the gait of his paragraphs you never see the effort of the muscles, but only their easy play. The surface is so smooth that the volume of the current is at first not perceived. With him words and sentences make a transparent plate-glass which lets in a world of light and landscape, itself invisible. In the best speeches and orations of Daniel Webster, through compactness with lucidness of statement, and purity and limpidity of diction and style, we have another shining illustration of power well clothed and concealed. Mr. Webster, besides having more of other qualifications for making an enduring speech than almost any other forensic or legislative speaker that ever spoke, is more of an artist in his logical and oratorical work than any other: he is more organic, with a higher sense of the beautiful.

Joubert had the soul of a poet: he was easily set aglow by the tender and the beautiful: his sensibilities were purged by a celestial fire. In poetry as in all literature, he sought the essential, looking inward with a penetrating vision. Here is a striking passage on the relation between sense and sound: " Say what we will, it is above all, the meaning which makes the sound and the harmony; and as in music it is the ear that flatters the mind, in speech it is through the mind that the ear is flattered. Bating a small number of words that are either very rough or very smooth, languages are made up of words the sound of which is indifferent, and the agreeableness of which, even for the ear, is determined by the sense. For example, in the line of Boileau,—

" Traçat à pas tardifs un pénible sillon,"

we notice hardly or not at all the bizarre juxtaposition of all these syllables, — *tra-ça-ta-pas-tar;* so true it is that the sense makes the sounds." There are people whose musical ear is finite, who can take in a march, or a waltz, or a ballad, or even a *bra-*

vura, but who are baffled by a symphony of Beethoven. So there are readers of poetry whose ear is more metrical than rhythmic, and who thence — metre being verbal and rhythm spiritual — look more to the measured sequence and outward quality of words than to their drift and inward spirit. They cannot hear deep enough for the music that is made by a fresh poetic incarnation through the marriage of thoughtfulness with tenderness.

Joubert was one of those who grow wiser with years, and the number who do so is not large ; for wisdom is not the fruit of mere age, but is a spirit which reason distils from the juices wherewith the years get to be saturated from the long flow of good feeling. Joubert ripened to the last without withering. As his body grew old its strength, to use one of his own phrases, " shifted its place and retired into his mind." For him " the winter of the body was the autumn of the soul ; " and so of old age he writes with genial cheerfulness.

Among the distinguished gifts whose union makes him a man and author so rarely excellent and attractive, the truthfulness of Joubert's nature takes highest rank. In human achievements, in whatever province, truthfulness is the centre round which the other mental agencies group themselves. In philosophy as in statesmanship, in literature as in business, in theology as in physics, in all things whereon and wherewith the mind of man can act, not truth merely, but *the spirit of truth*, is the power primarily needful, — as needful as its kernel to the peach, as oxigen to air. Without it, there may be temporary triumph, but never a final success.

The volume of "Thoughts" opens with a preliminary chapter, entitled *The author depicted by himself*. Of this chapter the contents are, like those of the others, in detached paragraphs or sentences. Such of these as seem most suitable for translation find here their fitting place. The reader will, however, understand them better and enjoy them more, after he shall have become acquainted with the writer of them through study of the other chapters.

"I have given my flowers and my fruit: I am now nothing but a hollow trunk ; but whoever sits in my shade and listens to me grows wiser. -

"In many things I am like the butterfly: like

him I love the light; like him I there consume my life; like him I need, in order to spread my wings, that there be fair weather about me in society, and that my mind feel itself surrounded and as if penetrated by a mild temperature, that of indulgence.

" I need to be shone on by looks of favor. Of me it is true to say : *he who pleases is king; he who does not please is nothing.* I go where I am desired at least as willingly as where I go to please myself.

" I quit Paris unwillingly, because I must part from my friends; and I quit the country unwillingly, because I must part from myself.

" *Philanthropy and repentance is my motto.*

" I dislike prudence unless it be moral. I have a bad opinion of the lion since I have learnt that his step is oblique.

" When my friends are blind of one eye, I look at them in profile.

"I desire neither a mind without light, nor a mind without bandage. To be happy in life we require to be able bravely to blind ourselves.

"Instead of complaining that the rose has thorns, I congratulate myself that the thorn is surmounted by roses, and that the bush bears flowers.

"There is no *bon ton** without a slight contempt for others. Now it is impossible for me to despise any one entirely unknown to me.

"I can sow, but I cannot build and found.

---

* I leave the French phrase untranslated; for rendered into English by *good manners*, the judgment conveyed by the words would assuredly be unsound. Even as they stand, the opinion of Joubert may be gainsaid; for although the phrase *bon ton* applies to the demeanor aimed at in the aristocratic circles of Europe, where necessarily prevails a jealous and exclusive spirit, the best bred in those circles have no need, in their bearing, of an infusion of so uncongenial and unchristian an element as contempt, the best breeding being the fruit of a humane sympathetic spirit, made graceful and winning by the unconscious agency of an innate sense of the beautiful. To Joubert's judgment is to be preferred one given by a refined critic on " Horace," in the 33d number of the (London) "National Review," who says, "*bonhomie* (kindliness) is an invariable accompaniment of the highest breeding."

" I have never learnt to speak ill, to revile, and to curse.

" The pain of dispute exceeds by much its utility. All disputation makes the mind deaf; and when people are deaf I am dumb.

" I call not reason that brutal reason which crushes with its weight what is holy and what is sacred ; that malignant reason which delights in errors when it can discover them ; that hard and scornful reason that insults credulity.

" The goodness of others gives me as much pleasure as my own.

" My discoveries (and each one has his own), have brought me back to prejudices.

" When I shine I consume myself.

" I shall have dreamt the beautiful, as people say they dream happiness. But mine is a better dream, for even death and its prospect, far from breaking its continuity, give it more scope.

"The ways suited to confidence are familiar to me, but not those that are suited to familiarity.

"Like Montaigne, I am unfit for continuous discourse.

"I am like an Æolian harp, which gives out some fine sounds, but executes no air.

"My mind likes to range through boundless spaces, and to sport in floods of light, where it perceives nothing, but where it is filled with joy and brightness. And what am I? Only an atom in a ray.

"I am like the poplar, that tree which always looks young, even when it is old.

"Madame Victorine de Chatenay said of me, that I seemed to be a soul that by accident had met with a body, and tries to make the best of it. I cannot deny that this was well said.

"Like the lark, I like to wander far, and above my nest.

"Long have I endured the torments of a fertility which cannot find expression.

"I do not like philosophy, and especially not metaphysics, either biped or quadruped: I like it winged and songful.

"You arrive at truth through poetry, and I arrive at poetry through truth.

"One may have tact early, and taste very late; this was the case with me.

"There are few pictures that I like, few operas, few statues, few poems, and yet I am very fond of the Fine Arts.

"I have too much brain for my head; it cannot play at ease in its case.

"I have many forms of ideas, but too few forms of words.

"The Revolution drove my mind from the world of reality by making it too horrible for me.

" I wished to do without words and despised them: they revenge themselves by their difficulty.

" If there be a man plagued with the accursed ambition of putting a whole volume into a page, a whole page into a sentence, and that sentence into a word, it is I.

" In verse the attention is held by the amusement of the ear. Prose has not this resource; could it have it? I am making trial; but I think not.

" I like to see two truths at once. Every good comparison gives the mind this advantage.

" It is not my sentence that I polish, but my thought. I pause until the drop of light that I need is formed and falls from my pen.

" I should like to have wisdom coined, that is, struck into *maxims*, into *proverbs*, into *sentences*, easy to retain and to circulate. Why can I not cry down and banish from the language of men, like an adulterated currency, those words that they misuse and that deceive them.

"I had need of age to learn what I wished to know, and I should have need of youth to say well what I know.

"Heaven gave strength to my mind but for a time, and that time is passed.

"Men are accountable for their actions; but for me, it is of my thoughts that I shall have to give an account. They serve not only as foundation to my work but to my life.

"My thoughts! it is the house to lodge them in that is so hard for me to build."

Joubert not having published his volume, or prepared it for publication, to him was denied the privilege of elimination, of final rejection, — a privilege precious to authors, and especially to one so refined and exacting as he was. Among his papers was found a scrap, which proves that the fruits of meditation that had seemed ripe enough to be laid away in manuscript, were deemed by him, in his latter years, wholesome enough to be given to the public. This fragment reads as follows : " If I die and leave some scattered thoughts on important subjects, in the name of humanity I conjure those who shall become the depositaries of them, to suppress nothing that does not accord with current opinion. During my life I loved only truth ; I have reason to think that I have seen it on many great subjects ; perhaps, one of those sentences that I shall have put forth in haste . . . . . " Like all men who, from insight and power, are original, Joubert was not in accord with current opinion ; originality involving, indeed, divergence from the beaten track. In the above fragment he, however, probably refers not to those of his " thoughts " that are the newest and deepest and most original, but to those that were the offspring of a repugnance in him to the seeming lawlessness and godlessness of the new ideas and opinions of his time. The mental expansion which preceded the French Revolution and caused it, that he could have enjoyed and aided ; but the frenzies and distractions, which were the tempest, only through which could equilibrium be restored in a moral and political atmosphere so abnormal and vicious as was that of France, alarmed and saddened him, and made " the world of reality too horrible," and thus brought him " back to prejudices," which, however, could not stiffen to uncharitableness in the heavenly atmosphere made for him by himself out of his own heart. Moreover, a man of delicate organization, who has been early bound by the bonds and bands of dogmatic theology, has difficulty in mastering and accepting the idea of indefinite development. Thence Joubert, horror-struck and thrown back on himself, looked upon his countrymen as wild beasts who could only be saved by being re-chained, not as men who, in rending the tight folds of long regal and ecclesiastical despotism, smote about them for a time madly and disastrously.

In selecting from the " Thoughts " I have sought those that are the largest and deepest, that are the least one-sided or partial, those that combine originality with beauty, brevity with weight, freshness with truth ; and thence I have passed over most of those that were written under dogmatic influences, and which, therefore, seem to me partial or one-sided. At the same time, to any who shall find themselves profited by what is here given them in English, may be cordially recommended the original volume, of which scarcely the half is here translated.

The volume proves how inexhaustible are the resources of the human mind. After Pythagoras, Epictetus, Marcus Aurelius, the Imitation, Pascal, Rochefoucauld, La Bruyère, here are embodied in sententious form, novel insights, fresh inspirations, original judgments, on familiar things and authors. A fine, firm intellect carries in its grasp a light, kindled at the flame of a soul so profound and pure, that new illumination is cast on old things, and new aspects are revealed.

Such refined affluence as the volume of Joubert exhibits could only come from a tender, noble, full nature. The book has in it the life, or rather a distilment from the life, of a good, intellectual man of genius. More than other men, far more than most men, Joubert lived in the silent, boundless, infinite domain of the inward; a domain in him irradiated by hope, love, and the beautiful. He questioned, and analyzed, and fed on his intuitions, his interior promptings, his soul-movements. In a letter to Madame de Beaumont he says: "To live is to think, and to feel one's soul: all the rest, drinking, eating, etc., however much I may make of them, are but the preparations for living, the means for sustaining life." But he was no recluse: that soul that he loved to feel, others felt: his life was a central warmth that radiated warmth to a wide circle. He was full of sympathies, full of affections. His experience had been wide and rich. " My soul," he says, " inhabits a place through which all the passions have passed: I have known them all." In the flower of his manhood the tempest of the French Revolution had gone over him; but from the delicate chords of his susceptive soul had drawn only notes of wail, and piety, and faith. Through those dark and terrible years his life runs like a thread of light, at first illuming his own path, then partly recognized as a guide by others, and now, long after his decease, in these emanations from his generous, subtle, spiritual being, his " Thoughts," shining with inextinguishable lustre and beauty, to be for his fellow-men a precious possession forever.

THOUGHTS OF JOUBERT.

I.

Of God, Creation, Eternity, Piety, Religion.

GOD is so great, so vast, that, in order to comprehend him, we are obliged to divide him.

In this process of imagining God, the first means is the human figure, the last term is light, and, in light, splendor. I know not that the imagination can go farther; but the mind goes on when the imagination stops; to the mind space, omnipotence, infinity present themselves — a circle delightful to describe and which is ever recommencing. We quit it, we return to it, we dive into it, we come out of it. What signifies that everybody completes it? Our duty, our happiness is to keep in it and not to trace it.

We know God through piety, — the only mood of our soul through which he is placed within our reach and can show himself to us.

We always believe that God is like ourselves: the indulgent affirm him indulgent; the stern terrible.

Every thing that is very spiritual, and wherein the soul has truly a part, recalls us to God, to piety. The soul cannot move, wake, open its eyes, without feeling God. We feel God with the soul, as we feel the air with the body.

Dare I say it? We know God easily, provided we do not constrain ourselves to define him.

We comprehend the earth only when we have known heaven. Without the spiritual world the material world is a disheartening enigma.

All that presents to man a spectacle of which he can ascertain neither the cause nor the limits, leads him to the idea of God, — that is, of him who is infinite.

The God of metaphysics is but an idea; but the God of religions, the Creator of heaven and earth, the Sovereign Judge of actions and of thoughts, is a power.

The universe obeys God, as the body obeys the soul that fills it.

The world was made as is the web of the spider: God drew it from his bosom, and his will span it, unrolled it, spread it. What we call nothingness is his invisible plenitude; his power is a ball, but a substantial ball, containing an inexhaustible whole, which, ever a winding off, remains ever entire. To create the world a grain of matter sufficed; for all that we see, this mass which affrights us, is nothing but a grain which the Eternal has created and set to work. By its ductility, by the hollows which it enfolds and the art of the workman, it presents, in the embellishments that have issued out of it, a kind of immensity. Every thing seems to us full: every thing is empty, or to speak more truly, every thing is hollow. The elements themselves are hollow: God alone is full. But this grain of matter, where was it? It was in the bosom of God, as it is there now.

"Nothing is made out of nothing;" but the sovereign power of God is not nothing: it is the source of matter as well as of spirit.

God multiplies intelligence, which communicates itself, like fire, *ad infinitum*. Light a thousand torches at one touch, its flame remains always the same.

Let us be men with men, and always children before God; for in his eyes we are but children. Old age itself, in presence of eternity, is but the first moment of a morning.

We should speak to men of destruction only to make them think of duration, and of death only to make them think of life; for death runs into life and destruction precipitates itself into duration.

The anger of God is of a moment: his pity is eternal.

In the moral world nothing is lost, as in the material world nothing is annihilated. All our thoughts and all our sentiments here below are but the beginning of sentiments and thoughts that will be finished elsewhere.

Whither go our ideas? They go into the memory of God.

We must betake ourselves to Heaven; all things are there in their types, all truths, all pleasures, whereof we have here below but the shadows. Such is the supreme beauty of this world, that only to name well what is in it, or even to designate it with exactness, would suffice to form a beautiful style and to make a beautiful book.

It seems to me that in the far future of another life, they will be the happiest who will not have had in their existence a single moment which they cannot recall with satisfaction. Up there, as down here, our memories will be an important part of our good and of our ill.

Heaven is for those who think of it.

Piety is a sublime wisdom, which surpasses all others, a kind of genius, which gives wings to the mind. No one is wise who is not pious.

Piety is a kind of modesty. It makes us cast down our thoughts, just as modesty makes us cast down our eyes, in presence of whatever is forbidden.

Piety is the only means of escaping the dryness which the labor of reflection causes in the sources of our sensibilities.

Piety draws us to what is most powerful, which is God, and to what is most weak, as children, the aged, the poor, the sick, the unhappy, the afflicted. Without piety, old age offends the sight, infirmity repels, imbecility shocks us. With it, we see in old age only long life, in infirmity suffering, in imbecility misfortune : we feel only respect, compassion, and the desire to relieve.

Charity is a species of piety. In its presence repugnances are to such a degree overcome, that one may say, for the pious, all afflictions have attraction.

God has put into man not only the love of himself, but also the love of others. The wherefore of the most of our qualities is, that we are good, that we are men, that we are the work of God.

To love God, and to make ourselves loved by him; to love our fellows, and to make ourselves loved by them: this is morality and religion; in both, love is every thing: end, beginning, and means.

God wishes us to love even his enemies.

To think of God is an action.

We should love God's gifts and denials, love what he wishes and what he does not wish.

God loves the soul, and as there is an attraction which carries the soul to God, there is one, if I dare so speak, which carries God to the soul. He makes of the soul his joy.

Forgetfulness of the things of earth, and intent thought on the things of heaven; exemption from all eagerness, from all care, from all trouble and from all effort; fulness of life without any agitation; the joys of sentiment without the labor of thought; the raptures of ecstasy without preliminary meditation; in a word, pure spirituality in the bosom of the world and amid the tumult of the senses: it is but the bliss of a minute, a moment; but that moment of piety sheds suavity over our months and over our years.

True religion is the poetry of the heart: it has enchantments useful to our manners; it gives us both happiness and virtue.

Religion is neither a theology, nor a theosophy; it is more than all that: a discipline, a law, an indissoluble engagement.

Without dogma,* morality is only maxims and sentences; with dogma, it is precept, obligation, necessity.

We should yield to Heaven and resist men.

We judge ourselves according to the judgment of men, instead of judging ourselves according to the judgment of Heaven. God is the only mirror

---

* Dogmas are of man, and if sound are a good scaffolding; but if made the permanent support of God's building, the soul, they weaken and disfigure it.

in which we can know ourselves; in all the others we only see ourselves.

May it not be said that since the advent of Jesus Christ, God has infused into nature more light and more grace? It seems, indeed, that since that time there has been in the world a more general knowledge of all duties and a more diffused facility to practise the true virtues and all the great virtues.

Incredulity is only a form of being of the mind; but impiety is a vice of the heart. This sentiment is made up of horror of what is divine — scorn of men, and contempt for amiable simplicity.

Shut your eyes and you will see.

Our soul is ever fully alive. It is so in the sick, in those who have fainted, in the dying: it is still more alive after death.

One must be religious with naturalness, self-forgetfulness, kindliness,* and not with dignity and a high-bred air, not gravely and mathematically.

When devotion is not accompanied by humility, it inevitably becomes pride.

* Avec naïveté, abandon et bonhomie.

God illumines those who think often of him, and who lift their eyes toward him.

The best prayers are those which have nothing distinct, and which thus partake of simple adoration. God listens but to thoughts and sentiments. Inward words are the only ones he hears.

We should ask for virtue urgently and at any cost, and prosperity timidly and with resignation. To ask is to receive, when we ask for a genuine good.

Can it be that there is aught superior to faith — a sight, a vision? Can there flash from above some ray that should give more light to certain men than to certain others? And, during the broad day of life, will God, from out the dark, deep cloud, manifest himself to some few? But even if that could be, who would dare to flatter himself that he had had this illumination?

II.

The Chapters.* (Les Chapitres.)

I.

GOD is God; the world is a place; matter is an appearance; the body is moulded by the soul; man's earthly life is a beginning.

All beings come from little, and little is wanting but that they come from nothing. An oak is born of an acorn, a man of a drop of water. And in this acorn, in this drop of water, how many superfluities! Every germ occupies but a point. The too much contains the enough, and is its necessary place and indispensable aliment, at least in its beginnings. No one should suffer the too much in himself, but we must love it in the world; for nowhere would there be enough of any thing if in some place there were not always a little too much of every thing.

> * The significance of this heading is not obvious. The soaring paragraphs which come under it deserve, from their spirituality and beauty, a unique designation; and Joubert may have purposed, by the name he has prefixed to them, to indicate that they are such a condensation of his thoughts on Deity, that each section contains the pith of a chapter. His other headings he terms *titres*.

II.

Truth consists in conceiving or imagining persons or things as God sees them; and virtue consists in giving one's self goodness; and goodness, if it is perfect, in having only those sentiments which we may believe an angel would have, if, having become what we are, while remaining all that he is, he were put in our place and saw what we see.

Wisdom is repose in light; but it is light itself that often excites wisdom to sport in its beams, by the day it diffuses and the illusions it causes, coloring abstractions like light clouds, and giving to the obvious a glow of serenity.

There is naught beautiful but God; and, after God, what is most beautiful is the soul; and after the soul, thought; and after thought, speech. Thence, the more a soul is like God, the more a thought is like a soul, and the more a word is like a thought, the more beautiful is each.

III.

Here are graver thoughts; I will speak more gravely.

The will of God depends on his wisdom, on his goodness, on his justice, and these are the only bounds of his power. Whatever is evil will be punished; whatever is good will be set down, and nothing will be exacted but what shall have been possible.

The love of bodies separates souls from God, for the love of bodies is not for God. The horror of evil unites to God, for God has a horror of evil. But he loves all souls, even those that love evil, if, at the bottom of their aberrations, they preserve some love of him and some abhorrence of themselves. What we love in spite of ourselves, through the strength of matter, we should not love from choice, or with consent, for then we should love it too much, and therein would be the evil.

To establish the reign of God, or the existence of all good, is the law of politics, or of the government of nations, and that of economy, or of the government of the house, and it is likewise the law of morals, or of the government of self. Law is that which obliges, and from whose obligation there is no escape, not even through the goodness of God.

IV.

I resume my joy and my wings, and fly to other realms of light.

An object, whatever it be, is more or less agreeable to us, according as it is, in all points, more or less clearly similar to its type or its model, which is in the ideas of God. Our qualities are more or less praiseworthy, and even more or less real, more or less eminent, more or less worthy of their name, according as they are, in their action and their essence, more or less conformable to their law, whereof God has the idea.

In truth, we see every thing in God, and we see nothing but in him, at least in metaphysic. Without his idea and his ideas, we can perceive nothing, distinguish nothing, explain nothing, and, least of all, rate any thing at its intrinsic value, at that secret holy value which, placed in the bosom and at the centre of each thing, like an epitome of itself, is all that precisely marks, when read by this light, the exact degree of merit of each, its true weight, and its just price.

v.

In matter nothing pleases us but what is almost spiritual, as its emanations; but what almost touches the soul, as perfumes and sounds; but what has the air of an impression left on it by some intelligence, as the festoons that embroider and the designs that are carved on it; but what gives illusion, as forms, colors; in short, but what in matter seems to have issued out of a thought, or to have been arranged for some purpose, showing a will. Thus, in the solidities about us, we can only love what they have that is mobile; and, in what is subtle, we owe our most tender pleasures to what has scarcely an existence, to those vapors that are more than light, and to those invisible undulations which, by penetrating us, lift us higher and further than our senses. Pressed against and pushed by bodies, we are, in reality, only reached by the spirit of things, to such a degree are we ourselves spirit.

VI.

I said well : matter is an appearance; all is little, and nothing is much; for what is the entire world ? I have thought on it, I almost see it, I believe it, and I will say it boldly. The entire world is but a little condensed ether, the ether but a little space, and space but a point, which was endued with the power to display a little space, when it should be developed, but which had scarcely any, when God sent it forth from his bosom. Newton himself said it: "When God wished to create the world, he commanded a bit of space to become and to remain impenetrable." With its gravitations, its attractions, its impulsions, and all those blind forces with which the learned make so much noise, with the enormous masses that frighten our eyes, the whole of matter is only a particle of metal, a grain of glass made hollow, a water-bubble, where play light and shade ; in short, a shadow, where nothing presses but on itself, nothing is impenetrable but to itself, attracts or but retains itself, and seems stout and vast but to the extreme exiguity, to the infinite littleness of the particles of this whole, which is almost nothing. All this world, when the hand of God poises it, what weight has it? When the look of God embraces it, what extent has it? When he sees it, how does it look to him? And when he penetrates into it, what does he find? This is the question. The most terrible of imaginable catastrophes, the conflagration of the universe, what could it be but the crackle, the sparkle, and evaporation of a grain of powder in a candle.

O truth! only souls and God offer grandeur and consistency to thought, when thought returns into itself, after having traversed everywhere, sounded every thing, tried every thing in its crucibles, refined every thing in its light and in the light of the sky, searched into every thing, known every thing.

III.

OF MAN, OF ORGANS, THE SOUL AND THE INTELLECTUAL FACULTIES.

WE see every thing through ourselves. We are a medium always interposed between things and us.

The body is a tent in which our existence is encamped.

In the face there is something luminous which is not found in other parts of the body.

In the eyes there is intellect, soul, and body.

The voice is a human sound which nothing lifeless can perfectly imitate. It has an authority and a property of insinuation which writing wants. It is not merely air, it is air modulated by us, impregnated with our warmth, and, as it were, enveloped in the haze of our atmosphere, from which an emanation attends it, and which gives it a certain configuration and certain virtues fitted to act on the mind. Speech is thought incorporated.

Man is born with the faculty of speech. Who gave it to him? He who gives its song to the birds.

In languages there is something fatidical and inspired.

The soul is an illuminated vapor which burns without being consumed; our body is its lantern. Its flame is not only light, but feeling.

The soul is to the eyes what sight is to the touch: it seizes what escapes all the senses. As, in art, that which is most beautiful is beyond prescription, so, in knowledge, what is most high and most true is beyond experience.

In the soul there is a taste that loves good, as in the body there is an appetite that loves pleasure.

The intellect is the atmosphere of the soul.

The more I think on it, the more I see that the intellect is something outside of the soul, as the hands are outside of the body, the eyes outside of the head, the branches outside of the trunk. It helps to *do* more, but not to *be* more.

The mind is a fire whose flame is thought.

I suspect that the organs of thought are divided into several classes.* By some we imagine, by others we reflect, so, however, that no one of them is moved without moving the others. Men of great genius are those whose organs have such strength and such union, that they are always moved together in an exact proportion.

We can conceive no object without previously conceiving its possibility; no individual, without previously a nature; no existence, without previously an existence; nothing in short individual without a universal idea. The universal idea is the place that is indispensable in order that each thing fix itself in our mind. It is as a primary idea that comes to us from our mind, from nature and from God himself: a notion mathematical, transcendent, which precedes all learning and even all experience. When you say: God is just, God is good, what do you, if not one of the highest and boldest operations of the mind? You compare God to a model, his being to an ideal nature. You ascribe to him a perfection which you conceive in some manner out of himself; to such a degree is the primary out of existence to the understanding, existing only in essence! And this high, this bold

---

* About the time, probably, that Joubert wrote this, Gall was just entering on his career of splendid discovery, whereby was demonstrated the truth of Joubert's intuition.

operation, the most insignificant mind performs it constantly, without effort, nay, inevitably. Ideas! Ideas! they are before all, and precede all in our mind.*

Is there any thing better than judgment? Yes: the gift of insight, the eye of the mind, the instinct of penetration, the prompt discernment, in short, the natural sagacity to discover all that is spiritual.

Intellect is the florescence, the complete development of the germ of the human plant.

Imagination is the eye of the soul.

I call imagination the faculty of rendering sensuously perceptible what is intellectual, of incarnating what is spirit; in a word, of making visible, without distortion, what is of itself invisible.

It is to imagination that the greatest truths are revealed: for example, Providence, its march, its purposes; they escape our judgment; the imagination alone sees them.

* Like Coleridge, Joubert was a devout student of Plato, and some of the latter chapters of " The Friend " seem almost an amplification of this paragraph of Joubert. It is in one of these chapters that Coleridge calls Plato the Athenian Verulam and Bacon the British Plato.

Without imagination, sensibility is reduced to the moment in which we exist; the sensations are more vivid, shorter, and have no harmony in their succession.

IV.

OF THE NATURE OF MINDS.

WE measure minds by their stature; it would be better to estimate them by their beauty.

Minds are like fields: in some, what is best is the surface; in others, it is the bottom, at a great depth.

The tendency towards good, the quickness to grasp it, and the constancy in wishing it; the intensity, suppleness, and tenacity of the springs which this tendency puts into play; the liveliness, force, and precision of the efforts towards the end aimed at, are the elements which, like so many letters, form, by their combinations, the intrinsic gauge of the man and determine his value.

Nature has made two kinds of excellent minds: the one to produce beautiful thoughts and beautiful actions, the other to admire them.

Heaven rarely grants to the same men the gift of thinking well, of speaking well, and of acting well, in all things.

Every mind has its dregs.

There is a weakness of body which proceeds from the strength of the mind, and a weakness of mind which comes from the strength of the body.

The mind has strength, so long as one has the strength to complain of its weakness.

There is always some levity even in excellent minds: they have wings to rise, and also to stray.

Some find activity only in repose, and others repose only in movement.

As there are men who have more memory than judgment, there are some who, in a manner, have more thoughts than intellect, and so can neither harness them nor drive them. Others have not thoughts enough for their intellect, so that it wastes away of *ennui*, if not enlivened by trifles. Others, in short, have too many thoughts for their age and for their health, and are plagued by them.

A man is never mediocre when he has much good sense and much good feeling.

To be interested in small things as in great, to be apt and ready for the one as for the other, is not weakness and littleness, but capacity and sufficiency.

The mind should be allowed to dwell only on thoughts that are happy, satisfying, or perfect. Happy thoughts! We have them when we expect them, and are in a state to receive them.

There are minds of which it may be said, It is light in them; and of others, only, It is warm. There is much warmth where there is much movement, and much light where there is much serenity. Without serenity, no light.

To be enlightened : a big phrase! Certain men think themselves enlightened because they are decided; thus taking conviction for truth, and strong conception for intelligence. There are others who, because they know all the words, think they know all the truths. But who is enlightened with that eternal light which cleaves to the sides of the brain, and makes eternally luminous the minds into which it has entered, and the objects it has touched ?

There are minds that are like convex or concave mirrors, which represent objects just as they receive them, but which never receive them such as they are.

There are men who, when they speak on some subject or form a judgment, look into their head, instead of looking into God, into their soul, into their conscience, into the bottom of things. You perceive this habit of their mind in their expression and the direction of their eyes.

False minds are those that, without having the feeling of the true, have its definitions; who look into their brain, instead of looking before them; who, in their deliberations, consult the notions they have of things, and not things themselves.

Falseness of mind comes from falseness of heart; it proceeds from one's having secretly for aim one's own opinion, and not the true opinion. The false mind is false in every thing, as a squinting eye looks always obliquely.

In certain minds there is a nucleus of error which attracts and assimilates every thing to itself.

Sometimes great minds are, nevertheless, false minds. They are well-constructed compasses, but whose needles, affected by some neighboring object, always turn from the north.

It is not a strong head but a strong reason that we should honor in others and desire for ourselves.

OF THE NATURE OF MINDS.

Often what is called a strong head is only a strong unreason.

There are heads that have no windows, and that daylight cannot strike from above. Nothing comes into them from the side of Heaven.

Few minds are spacious; few even have a vacant place in them. Almost all have capacities that are narrow and occupied by some knowledge which stops them up. To enjoy itself and let others enjoy it, a mind should ever keep itself larger than its own thoughts.

There are minds meditative and hard to please, that in their labors are distracted by immense perspectives and far glimpses of the celestial beautiful, some image or ray of which they would like to put everywhere, because they have it always in sight, even when they have nothing before their eyes; minds that are the friends of light, and which, when they get an idea that can be turned to account, consider it long and wait until it shines, according to the saying of Buffon, when he defined genius the aptitude for patience; minds that have learnt by experience that the most barren matter and the very tamest words bear in their bosom the principle and possibility of some lustre, like those hazel-nuts of the fairies, wherein diamonds were found by those who had lucky hands; minds that are persuaded that this beauty of which they are enamored, beauty pure and elementary, is diffused in all points that thought can reach, as fire in all bodies; minds wakeful and penetrating, that see this fire in the pebbles of all literature, and can disengage themselves from those that fall into their hands only after having for a long time sought for the vein that concealed it, and having made it suddenly flash from them; minds that have also their systems, and that pretend, for example, that to see all things as beautiful, is to see and exhibit each thing such as it really is in the recesses of its being, and not such as it exists to the eyes of the inattentive, who only look at surfaces; minds that are not easily satisfied, on account of a perspicacity which makes them see too clearly both the models that should be followed and those that should be avoided : minds active, although dreamy, that can only rest in solid truths, nor be happy but through the beautiful, or, at least, through those divers charms which are minute particles of it and nimble sparkles; minds much less in love with glory than with perfection, that seem to be idle and are the most busy, but which, because their art is long and life is always short, unless some happy chance puts at their disposal a subject wherein is found in superabundance the element whereof they have need and room for their ideas, live little

OF THE NATURE OF MINDS. 57

known, and die without a monument, having obtained as their portion, amid excellent minds, only an inward fecundity which was known to few.*

* In this subtle, thoughtful, individualizing passage Joubert depicts himself.

V.

OF THE PASSIONS AND THE AFFECTIONS OF THE SOUL.

THE passions should be purged; all may become innocent, if they are well directed and moderated. Even hatred may be a commendable feeling when it is caused by a lively love of good. Whatever makes the passions purer makes them stronger, more durable, and more enjoyable.

We use up in the passions the stuff that was given us for happiness.

Passions are but nature; it is the not repenting that is corruption.

Repentance is an effort of nature which expels from the soul the principles of its corruption.

Remorse is the chastisement of crime; repentance is its expiation. The first belongs to a troubled conscience; the other to a soul changed for the better.

Men find motives of defiance in their ignorance

PASSIONS AND AFFECTIONS.

and in their vices, and motives of confidence in their knowledge and their virtues. Defiance is the portion of the blind.

All the passions seek that which nourishes them: fear loves the idea of danger.

Feeling renders insipid whatever is not itself; that is its inconvenience. It is also the great inconvenience of pleasure: it gets disgusted with reason.

Into every kind of excess there enters much coldness of soul: it is a thoughtful and voluntary abuse of pleasure.

Fear is the grace of excess.

Nothing belittles a man so much as petty pleasures.

The blind are cheerful, because their minds are not distracted from the representation of the things that can please them, and because they have more ideas than we have sights. This is a compensation granted them by Heaven.

Whatever occupies us about others cheers us; whatever only occupies us about ourselves saddens us. Hence the melancholy which besets a man who lives shut up in himself.

Cheerfulness clears the mind, especially literary cheerfulness. Dejection darkens it; extreme tension warps it; the sublime renews it.

Grace is in garments, in movements, in manners; beauty in the nude, and in forms. This is true of bodies; but when we speak of feelings, beauty is in their spirituality, and grace in their moderation.

Moderation consists in being moved as angels are moved.

God has commanded time to console the afflicted.

It is always our inabilities that irritate us.

Happiness is to feel that your soul is good; strictly speaking, there is none other, and this one can exist even in affliction. Hence it is that there are sorrows preferable to all joys, and which would be preferred to them by all who have experienced such sorrows.

Admit the covetous neither among thy friends nor among thy disciples, for they are incapable of wisdom and of fidelity.

Those who always love have not the leisure to complain and to be unhappy.

He who cannot see the beautiful side is a bad painter, a bad friend, a bad lover; he cannot lift his mind and his heart so high as goodness.

When we love, it is the heart that judges.

We always lose the friendship of those who lose our esteem.

A man who shows no defects is a fool or a hypocrite, whom we should mistrust. There are defects so bound to fine qualities that they announce them, defects which it is well not to correct.

Often our fine qualities are loved and praised only because our defects temper their lustre. It often even happens that we are loved rather for our defects than for our high qualities.

We should make ourselves loved, for men are only just towards those whom they love.

The punishment of those who have loved women too much is to love them always.

Tenderness is the repose of passion.

Good-will makes the enjoyments and the faculties of all the beings whom it embraces a party to its faculties and enjoyments. Man is an immense being who may exist, after a fashion, partially, but whose existence is the more delightful the more whole and full it is.

Whoever extinguishes in a man a feeling of good-will kills him partially.

Whatever multiplies the ties that bind man to man makes him better and happier.

The multitude of affections enlarges the heart.

Into the composition of every happiness enters the thought of having deserved it.

Ambition is pitiless: every merit that it cannot use is contemptible in its eyes.

We should keep our sentiments near the heart. When we accustom the heart to love what exists but for the mind, we have no ties but to abstractions, and to these we readily sacrifice realities. When we give so much love to men in the gross, we have none left to distribute in detail; all our good-will has been expended on the mass: individuals apply too late. These philosophical affections, which are not entertained without effort, dry up and destroy our capacity of loving.

No one is good, cannot be useful, deserves not to be loved, if he has not something heavenly, either in his intellect through thoughts, or in his will through affections directed upwards.

It is a great happiness, a great fortune, to be born good.

A part of goodness consists, perhaps, in esteeming and loving people more than they deserve; but then a part of prudence is to believe that people are not always worth what we rate them at.

Unless we keep watch on us, we shall find ourselves condemning the unfortunate.

The heart should walk before the intellect, and charity before truth.

Be gentle and indulgent to all; be not so to yourself.

Good impulses are naught, unless they become good actions.

To wish to do without our fellows, and to be

under obligation to no one, is a sure sign of a soul void of sensibility.

We should do good whenever we can, and do kindness at all times, for at all times we can.

The pleasure of giving is necessary to true happiness; but the poor may have it.

When you give, give with joy and in smiling.

Proud characters love those to whom they do a service.

We should endeavor, as much as possible, to despise no one.

By means of chastity the soul breathes a pure air in foulest places; by means of continency it is strong in whatever state the body may be. The soul is regal through its empire over the senses, beautiful by its light and its peace.

Ornaments were invented by modesty.

"God will punish," say the Orientals, "him who sees and him who is seen." Beautiful and terrible recommendation of modesty!

PASSIONS AND AFFECTIONS. 65

Eyes raised towards Heaven are always beautiful, whatever they be.

A certain modesty should be observed in wretchedness, grounded on that commendable and natural repugnance which all well-disposed people have to exhibit to the eyes of others objects that are disagreeable or repulsive. We should be very careful not to wound this virtuous feeling, in others or in ourselves. There are men whose benefactions do violence to misfortune; others whose complaints or countenance prostitute, in a measure, their misfortune to the passers-by. The poor should have the modesty of young virgins, who speak of their sex and their infirmities but with reserve, in secret, and from necessity.

A spider's web, made of silk and light, were not more difficult to execute than to answer this question, *What is modesty?*

VI.

WHAT IS MODESTY?

I HAVE to depict that which is charming, but which ever eludes the color of all the styles, and will hardly bear to be named. I here look at it from above, and it is grasped with difficulty, even when we contemplate it in ourselves or near us. My undertaking is, therefore, difficult; perhaps it is impossible. I ask that, at least, I be followed with perseverance in the labyrinth and circuities into which my path will lead me. I request to be left to move freely on the track whereon I am launched. In short, I claim for me what I myself have given to my subject and my language, — a patient hope and a long attention.

Modesty is an indescribable fear connected with our sensibility, which causes the soul, like the flower which is its image, to fold up and hide in itself, so long as it is delicate and tender, on the least appearance of what might wound it by too lively impressions or premature light. Hence that confusion which, arising at the sight of disorder, clouds and muffles our thoughts, and makes them, as it were, impervious to its hurts. Hence the tact put before all our perceptions, the instinct which resists whatever is forbidden, the motionless flight, the blind discernment, and the mute indicator of what should be avoided or should not be known. Hence that timidity which makes all our senses circumspect, and which preserves youth from risking its innocence, from stepping out of its ignorance, and of interrupting its happiness. Hence those startlings by which inexperience aims to remain inviolate, and flies what may please us too much, fearing what may wound it.

Modesty lowers our lids between our eyes and their objects, and places a still more effectual veil, a more marvellous guaze, between our mind and our eyes. The eye itself is sensible of it by a remoteness without distance and a magic background, which it lends to all our forms, to our voice, to our air, to our motions, and which give them so much grace. For we can easily see it; what its crystal is to the fountain, a glass to our pastels, its haze to the landscape, modesty is to beauty and to the least of our charms.

What is the import of Modesty? Wherefore was it given us? Of what use is it to the human soul? What is its purpose, and what its necessity? I am going to endeavor to explain.

When external nature wishes to create a visible being, so long as it has little solidity she uses precautions. She lodges it between tissues made of all substances, by means of an unknown mechanism, and prepares for it such a shelter that only the influence of life and motion can, without effort, penetrate therein. She places the embryo in repose, in solitude, in safety; finishes it slowly, and on a sudden brings it to light. Thus was formed the universe; thus are formed in us all our fine qualities.

When internal nature wishes to create our moral being, and cause to bloom in us some rare perfection, she first produces the germs of it, and deposits them in the centre of our existence, far from the agitations that disturb our surface. So long as we are too sensitive and are not finished, she makes us live in the shadow of a mysterious ornament, in order that the developments she is preparing may take place in safety in our coy capacities, and be not therein broken in upon by hard and strong passions — too naked impressions, such as other beings send forth, and which emanate from all bodies.

As the molecules, which cause our sensations, if they entered without retardation into this asylum, open to attack from every side, would destroy all that is most tender therein, by exposing the soul to the action of matter, nature erects against them a rampart. She surrounds with a circular, nonadhesive net-work, transparent and imperceptible, this loving, living alcove, where, sunk in a semi-slumber, the character in its germ receives all its accretions. Here she allows naught to penetrate but a twilight, a murmur, and the pure essence of all the affections. To all our sensations she opposes a reserve, and arms us with a supreme mechanism, which, to the visible integuments designed to guard from hurt our outward existence, superadds an invisible one, fitted to shield from pleasure our nascent sensibilities. At this epoch of life, in short, nature gives us an envelope: this envelope is modesty.

We can figure it to ourselves by imagining a circuit wherein our being is, in its budding season, isolated on all sides, and receives earthly influences through impediments that strip them of their refuse or absorb their excess. It arrests at our surface the useless sediments of impressions that arrive from without, and admitting into its recesses only their elementary part, divested of all superfluity, it makes the soul, without effort, acquire wisdom, and the will, the habit of obeying only impulses that are spiritual like itself. It secures to our faculties the time and the means of unfolding themselves without interference from without and without irregularity, in a circumscribed centre, where purity nourishes them and truth surrounds them like a transparent fluid. It keeps our hearts at rest and our senses without tumult, in its invisible bonds incapable of restraining us in our development, but capable of protecting us, by deadening all shocks and by opposing its barrier to our own ranges, when too much agitation might hurt or destroy us. It establishes between our senses and all their relations such a mediation and such intermediaries, that, by means of it, there can enter into the enclosure, where dwells the soul, only prepared images, measured emotions, and approved sentiments.

Need we now speak of its necessity? What is to the young of birds the white of the egg, and that web wherein their essence is contained; what is to the kernel its cap; what is its calyx to the flower, and the sky to the earth, that to our virtues is modesty. Without this preservative shelter, they could not blossom, their sanctuary would be violated, the germ laid bare, and the brood destroyed.

Let us apply this idea to facts, and the system to phenomena. We all have modesty, but not a like modesty. This immaterial web has divers textures. It is given to us all, but is not dispensed to us with an equal bounty, nor with the same favor. Some have a modesty wrought with little subtlety; others have but a rag of it. Only they who carry within them the germs of all perfections have a perfect modesty, a modesty that is whole, and whose countless threads are connected with all the points whither tends their existence. This is the one that I am describing.

We do not always keep it. It is like beauty: frightful accidents rob us of it, and of itself it quietly decreases and disappears, when it has become useless and that its end is attained. In short, modesty is in vigor so long as there is in us some unknown particle which has not taken on its substance and all its solidity, and until our organs have become susceptible of adopting and retaining eternal impressions. But when the soft seeds of our solid qualities are fully developed; when our first good impulses, like milk that coagulates, have ended in goodness, or that our natural goodness has become unchangeably fixed; when, nourished by chaste knowledge, our mind is unfolded, and can keep that equilibrium which we call reason, or that our reason is formed; when our moral integrity has insensibly acquired that indestructibility that we call character, or that character in its germ has received all its growth; in short, when the secret principle of any depravement being no longer able to introduce itself into us except through our will, and wound us except with our knowledge, our defence is in ourselves: then the man is completed, the veil drops, and the net is unwoven.

Even then, however, modesty stamps its mark upon us and leaves us its shield. We lose the mechanism of it, but we retain its virtue. There is left to us a last shadow of the web: I mean that blush which pervades and invests us, as if to efface the stain wherewith dishonor would infect us, or resist the excessive and unexpected pleasure which praise might cause us.

It bequeaths us still more precious fruits: a pure taste, whose first delicacy nothing has dulled; a bright imagination, whose polish nothing has blurred; a mind nimble and well-shaped, quick to rise to the sublime; a long flexibility, which no wrinkle has hardened; the love of innocent pleasures, the only ones that have been long known; the facility of being happy, through the habit of finding one's happiness in one's self; a something comparable to the velvet-down of flowers that have been long inextricably confined where no breath could enter; a charm borne in the soul, and which the soul applies to every thing, so that it loves incessantly and has the faculty of loving always; an eternal uprightness; for it must be avowed here that the soul is sullied by no pleasure which has passed through senses where has been leisurely deposited and slowly incorporated this incorruptibility; in short, such a habit of contentment with one's self, that one could no longer do without it, and that we must live irreproachable in order to live satisfied.

VII.

OF THE DIFFERENT AGES, OF LIFE, DISEASE, AND DEATH.

NOTHING is so hard to children as reflection. This is because the final and essential destination of the soul is to see, to know, and not to reflect. To reflect is one of the labors of life, a means of arriving, a road, a passage, and not a centre. To know and be known, — these are the two points of rest; such will be the happiness of souls.

Children tease and persecute whatever they love.

During our youth there is often something in us better than ourselves; I mean than our desires, our pleasures, our consents, our approbations. Our soul is then good, although our intellect and our will be not.

The younger are not within the line of duty when they have no deference for the older, nor the older, when they exact nothing from the younger.

Esteem the young man whom old men find polite.

Address yourself to young people; they know every thing.

There is an age when the forces of our body shift their place and retire into the mind.

The first and last portions of human life are the best of it, or at least the most respectable; the one is the age of innocence, the other the age of reason.

There is naught good in man but his young feelings and his old thoughts.

Two ages of life should have no sex: the child and the aged man should be as modest as women.

In clothes clean and fresh there is a kind of youth with which age should surround itself.

Old age takes from the man of sense only those qualities that are useless to wisdom.

It would seem that for certain mental productions the winter of the body is the autumn of the soul.

The residuum of human wisdom, refined by age, is perhaps the best there is in us.

The evening of life brings with it its lamp.

Old men are the majesty of a people.

Those who have a long old age are, as it were, purified of the body.

Politeness smoothes wrinkles.

We should cheer old men.

Old age was naturally more honored in times when people could not know much more than what they had seen.

With worn out senses and decreasing strength, we belong more to the life to come than to the present, and we are wretched if, no longer able to live on the one, we are at the same time unwilling to live on the other. By seeking to hold on, with hands that are powerless to grasp them, those goods that are escaping from us, we reject, we turn away from, those that are coming to us and seem, of their own accord, to give themselves to us, so well do they suit our weaknesses and accommodate themselves to them, through the small amount of strength and of life that are needed to enjoy them. At this epoch memory has lost its spring, and, by a signal beneficence, credulity is at its highest. Instead, then, of seeking to revive our memories, we should aim only to strengthen our hopes, to nourish them, to throw ourselves into them; for only for this are we any longer fit. Now, at this age, hopes can only have for their object the things of another life.

Time and health, when they change, change our task and our obligations. Every age is near its end; a future is ever near, which it behooves us all alike to be thinking of, — a future which youth has at its feet as old age has it before its eyes. Should we then act at the end of life as in its middle and at its beginning? At this epoch should not our action be otherwise directed than in other times? Should we then act for what is going, or for what is coming?

Life is a country which old men have seen and dwelt in. Those who are about to enter it cannot but apply to them to inquire about the routes.

We should receive the past with respect, and the present with distrust, if we wish to provide for the safety of the future.

Our life is woven wind.

How many people eat, drink, and marry; buy,

sell, and build; make contracts and nurse their fortune; have friends and enemies, joys and sorrows; are born, grow, live, and die, — but all the while asleep!

A little vanity and a little sensuality; of these are made up the life of most women and men.*

There are souls transparent and pure, whose life is like a sunbeam that sports in a drop of dew.

Every man is his own *Parcæ*, and weaves his future.

We should treat our life as we treat our writings: see that the beginning, the middle, and the end are in proportion, — in harmony. For this we need to make many erasures.

Debts shorten life.

The best of expedients for sparing ourselves trouble in life, is to think very little about our own interest.

---

* This should have been found on the page of Rochefoucauld, and not on that of Joubert; and had he himself prepared his "Thoughts" for publication, this one, and some others, would assuredly have been left in manuscript. It is one of those half-truths that are seen with half an eye. The whole eye sees deeper and takes in more.

OF LIFE, DISEASE, AND DEATH. 79

Forces always at work, — activity without rest, motion without intervals, agitations without calm, passions without melancholy, pleasures without tranquility! it is to banish sleep from life, to walk without ever sitting down, to grow old standing up, and to die without having slept.

This life is but the cradle of the other. What avail then sickness, time, old age, death, — different degrees of a metamorphosis which doubtless has here below only its beginnings.

VIII.

Of the Family and of Home, of Society, Conversation, Politeness, and Manners.

DOMESTIC sovereignty belongs to fathers over children, to masters over apprentices, and to old men over the young.

Few men are worthy to be heads of a family, and few families are capable of having a head.

There is a class of society where pious children know not that their parents are mortal. They have never dared to think of it.

We should choose for a wife only the woman we should choose for a friend, were she a man.

Nothing does so much honor to a woman as her patience, and nothing does her so little as the patience of her husband.

The triumph of women is not to wear out and conquer their persecutors, but to soften them and make them lay down their arms.

Children are well nursed only by their mothers, and men by their wives.

There are good qualities that are not transmitted, or that do not enter into the line of inheritance. What is delicate evaporates. The son of a grave and robust man is generally a man of sense; the son of a man of mind is seldom a man of mind.

The table is a kind of altar, which should be decked on holidays and festivals.

In temperance there is cleanliness and elegance.

A little of every thing, nothing to be had for the wishing it: great means of being moderate, of being discreet, of being contented.

The attention that is given to the house and to the furniture, draws the mind from the master, as the temple does from God.

We should wear our velvet next the skin; that is, show our amiability by preference to those with whom we live at home.

The aim of disputation and discussion should not be victory, but improvement.

It is never the opinion of others that displeases us, but the wish they sometimes have of imposing it upon us against our will.

The pleasure of pleasing is legitimate, and the desire to rule offensive.

We should pique ourselves on being reasonable, but not on being in the right; on sincerity, and not on infallibility.

We can only explain ourselves freely when we hope to be heard; and we can only hope to be heard by those who are half of our mind.

What can we make enter into a mind that is full, and full of itself?

In our head we should always keep a corner open and free, where we can make room for the opinions of our friends, and lodge them for a while. It becomes insupportable to converse with men in whose brain all the compartments are taken up, and where nothing can enter from without. Let us keep mind and heart hospitably open.

We should have within us that indulgence and that attention which make the thoughts of others bloom.

The attention of him who listens serves as accompaniment in the music of discourse.

It is better to make one's self acceptable than to make one's self important.

There are colloquies where neither the soul nor the body takes any part. Such I call those conversations in which no one speaks from the bottom of his heart, nor from the bottom of his humor; where there is neither unreserve, nor joyousness, nor effusion, nor play; where is found neither motion nor rest, neither distraction nor solace, neither thoughtfulness nor recreation; in short, where we have given nothing and received nothing, which is not a true intercourse.

Genuine witticisms surprise those who say them as much as those who listen to them; they arise in us in spite of us, or, at least, without our participation, — like every thing that is inspired.

You must not show a warmth that shall not be shared; nothing is colder than what is not communicated.

In the lightness of conversation we should respect modesty and piety. To make them blush, or to wound them, is a coarse play, a social crime.

It is better to stir a question without deciding it, than to decide it without stirring it.

One man likes to say what he knows, another to say what he thinks.

In the commerce of speech use only coin of gold and silver.

To make that ridiculous which is not so, is in some measure to make bad what is good.

Slander is the solace of malignity.

We may be pardoned for judging the living with our humor, but the dead we should judge only with our reason. Become immortal,* they can no longer be measured but with an immortal rule, — that of justice.

Politeness is the flower of humanity. He who is not polite enough is not human enough.

Politeness is a kind of anæsthetic which envel-

---

* The subtle, original Joubert here gives in to an unreasoning commonplace. Do we need the grave to make us immortal? Another much used phrase, to describe death by the gallows, is equally inaccurate. Of the executed culprit the newspapers say, "He was launched into eternity." We are launched into eternity the moment we are launched into life.

ops the asperities of our character, so that other people be not wounded by them. We should never be without it, even when we contend with the rude.

There is graciousness and a kind of urbanity in beginning with men by esteem and confidence. It proves, at least, that we have long lived in good company with others and with ourselves.

Politeness is to goodness what words are to thought. It tells not only on the manners, but on the mind and the heart; it renders the feelings, the opinions, the words, moderate and gentle.

Familiarity pleases, even without goodness; with goodness, it enchants.

Grace imitates modesty, as politeness imitates kindness.

Manners are an art. There are some that are perfect, others commendable, others faulty; but there are none indifferent. Why are there not among us precepts which teach them, or, at least, instruct us how to judge of them, as of sculpture and music. The science of manners would be more important to the happiness and virtue of men than we are disposed to believe.

IX.

Of Wisdom, Virtue, Morality, Rule, and Duty.

WISDOM is repose in light. Happy the minds that are high enough to sport in its beams.

Consult the ancients, listen to the aged. He is little wise who has only his own wisdom, and little learned is he who has only his own learning.

Imagination and wisdom combined are the charm of life and of art.

Wisdom is the strength of the weak.

Good sense accommodates itself to the world: wisdom endeavors to conform itself to Heaven.

Never cut what you can untie.

Virtue is the health of the soul. It gives relish to the smallest leaves of life.

His own virtue and the happiness of others, this is the twofold end of man on earth. His happiness is his supreme destination; but it is not what he should seek, it is only what he may expect and obtain, if he is worthy of it.

Virtue by calculation is the virtue of vice.

We are not innocent when we do harm to ourselves.

We should do every thing to let good people have their will.

Every thing can be learnt; even virtue.

Morality is the knowledge of those rules to which it is of moment to us to conform not only our actions, but also our affections. These are so important a portion of our mode of being, that I am astonished that no philosopher has embraced them within the definition of the essential object of morality. In fact, our affections are to our actions what ideas are to words. The essential point in morals, as in logic, is that the former be good.

Morality must have sky, as a picture air.

The morality of some people is in remnants, — never enough to make a coat.

Morality is a curb, not a spur.

Without a model, and without an ideal model, no one can do well.

A rule of conscience for one's self, a code of morals for one's self, a religion for one's self! By their nature, these things cannot be private.

A maxim is the exact and noble expression of an important and indisputable truth. Sound maxims are the germs of good: strongly imprinted in the memory, they nourish the will.

To think what we do not feel, is to lie to ourselves. Whatever we think, we should think with our whole being, will and body.

The end is not always given in order that it be attained, but to serve as a mark to aim at. For example, the precept to love our enemies.

He who lives without an object, at hap-hazard, as they say, has a dull life of it. In the moral life, to have enjoyment, we must have an aim and reach it. Now, whatever is aim is limitation. Not only is there no virtue where there is no rule and law, but there is not even pleasure. The very plays of children have laws, and would not exist without them; these laws are always a restraint, and, nevertheless, the more strictly they are obeyed the greater is the amusement.

In good times we are better than ourselves; in bad times, worse.

Without duty and its idea, no solidity in virtue.

Duty! In regard to ourselves, duty is independence of the senses, and, in regard to others, it is assiduity in help and support; help to well-being, to well-doing, to well-wishing; help through agreement and resistance, through gift and denial, through sternness and compliance, through praise and blame, through silence and speech, through pain and pleasure. Inhabitants of the same territory, fellow-travellers on the same road, we should all help one another; and, when we shall arrive at home, the first thing we shall have to do will be to give an account of what we shall have done for one another's weal, for happiness or virtue. Not a smile but we shall have credit for it.

As instruments we have a destination; as moral beings we have a liberty. Life and death, by which we enter the world or quit it; riches and property, which assign us a place in the world; glory and shame, elevation or abasement, which make us play a part in it; all these are dependent on the general march of human affairs, and make part of our destiny. God has reserved to himself the apportionment of them; to each individual he allots a share according to his will. Good and ill, on the contrary, are in our hands, or, as says the Scripture, in the hands of our counsel, because they make our merits and our demerits. Just then as our bodies are subject to two motions, that of the earth and our own, so are we governed by two wills, our own and that of Providence, — being authors of the one and instruments of the other; masters of our actions to merit the reward assigned to virtue, and machines for all the rest. To be better or worse depends on ourselves: all the rest depends on God.

Men must be either the slaves of duty, or the slaves of force.

Without duty, life is soft and boneless; it can no longer hold itself erect.

Always occupied with the duties of others, never with our own: Alas!

Happy are they who have a lyre in the heart, and in the mind a music which their actions execute! Their whole life will have been a harmony in unison with the eternal nomes.

X.

OF ORDER AND CHANCE, OF GOOD AND EVIL, OF TRUTH AND ERROR.

ORDER is the coördination of means to the end, of parts to the whole, of the whole to its destination, of action to duty, of work to the model, of reward to merit.

Well-being is the law of living bodies, but order is the law of minds.

Wherever there is no order and harmony, there is no longer the mark of God. There is desolation, and there has been degradation.

Think of the ills from which you are exempt.

The pleasure one feels at being just against one's self comes from a return to order through truth.

Sudden changes of fortune have a great inconvenience: the enriched have not learnt how to be rich, nor the ruined to be poor.

All are born to observe good order, but few are born to establish it.

It is impossible to sing and to dance in time without pleasure, so naturally agreeable is the observance of all true measure. Moral order is likewise measure and harmony; and so it is impossible to live well * without a secret and a very great enjoyment.

Success serves men as a pedestal; it makes them look larger, if reflection does not measure them.

There is but one way for the soul to escape from the ills of life: it is to escape from its pleasures and to seek enjoyment higher up.

We should concern ourselves about the ills and misfortunes of the world only to relieve them: to do nothing but contemplate and deplore them, is to embitter them to no purpose. He who broods on them with his eyes breeds tempests.

---

* No reader is likely to mistake here the meaning; but in our life so much does the material take precedence of the spiritual, that in common parlance the phrase, *to live well*, refers to meat and drink, and words that ought to be deep are made shallow. Were a traveller to write, "In Milan they live better than in Florence," to no reader would it occur that the moral life was better, but only that the kitchens and wine-cellars were better supplied.

Nor love nor friendship, nor respect nor admiration, nor gratitude nor devotedness, should make us lose the consciousness and the discernment of good and evil. This consciousness is a good which we are forbidden to part with, and which no price could pay.

In all things, whoever perverts the idea that men should form to themselves of perfection, perverts good at its source.

We should do good by good, and aim at it both in the means and in the end, both in the expedients and in the object. A good that has been done by means of evil is good that is marred, empoisoned, and will bring forth the evil whereof the germ has been placed in it: it is a stream which drains have fouled.

Perhaps, by a just disposition of Providence, crimes increase the evils they are intended to prevent. Perhaps, if Caligula had not been slain by a blow and a conspiracy which at first seem laudable, Claudius would not have reigned, nor Nero, nor Domitian, nor Commodus, nor Heliogabulus. Caligula, after some crimes, would have lived out his time, would have died in his bed, and the succession of Roman emperors would have taken another and a happier course. Perhaps what is evil, or infected with evil, produces never any thing but evil. God reserves in his hands calamities, to inflict them in due season. As for us, our duty is to do good, and nothing else — that is our task.

Truth! God alone sees it. What will be said, what will be thought, on high? therein consists truth. It consists in imagining things as God and the holy see them, as we see them beyond the world, when we cast thither our eyes. We see nothing in its true light, unless we see it from above. We should be able to say, That is true on earth, and it is true in heaven.

Write nothing, say nothing, think nothing which you do not believe to be true before God.

There are inferior truths, which do good service in life and its usages; medium truths, which exercise the mind and give it some satisfaction; and superior truths, which illuminate the soul, nourish it, and make its happiness. We should always connect the inferior to the superior by the medium.

What is true by the lamp is not always true by the sun.

Truth is like the sky, and opinion like clouds.

Our moments of light are moments of happiness: in the mind, when it is clear weather it is fine weather.

Time and truth are friends, although there are many moments that are opposed to truth.

When we knock in vain at the door of certain truths, we should try to get into them by the window.

A drop of light is better to give or to receive than an ocean of obscurities.

The joy caused by truth and beautiful thoughts makes itself felt in the words in which they are expressed.

Have a mind into which truth may enter naked, to issue from it attired.

Truth takes the character of the souls into which it enters. Rigorous and rough in arid souls, it is tempered and softened in loving souls.

They who never retract, love themselves more than truth.

We can get out of certain errors only at the

top; that is, by raising our minds above human things.

To be ever explaining the moral world by the physical is not safe, for in the physical we often take appearances for realities, and our conjectures for facts. We thus run the risk of having two errors instead of one, in applying to one world the false dimensions which we give to the other.

XI.

Of Philosophy, of Metaphysic, of Abstractions, of Logic, of Systems; of Space, of Time, of Light, of Air, etc.

I, *WHENCE, where, wherefore, how?* This is the whole of philosophy. Existence, origin, place, end, and means.

There is a philosophy full of flowers, of amenity, and of sportiveness, as sprightly as it is sublime.

As poetry is sometimes more philosophical than philosophy itself, metaphysic is, by its nature, more poetic than poetry.

Don't confound what is spiritual with what is abstract, and recollect that philosophy has a Muse, and ought not to be a mere reasoning laboratory.

What is to be done with that philosophy which banishes spirituality from the systems of the world, and piety from morals? It is just as if in a calculation we were to drop indispensable quantities, integral parts in an enumeration.

Metaphysic is a kind of poetry: devotion is its ode.

In good philosophy, the beautiful is always the most true, or, at least, the nearest to truth.

Metaphysic pleases the mind because the mind finds room in it; elsewhere it finds a *plenum*. The mind needs a world of fancy where it can move and range; it delights in it not so much on account of the objects as on account of the space which it finds there. It is thus that children like sand and water, and every thing that is fluid or flexible, because they can make of it what they will.

Practice is grave, but theory is cheering; the soul diverts and renews itself in the joys of intellect.

Religion is the only metaphysic that the multitude can understand and adopt.

Whoever does not feel what a different meaning should be given to the words *the beautiful* and *beauty*, *the true* and *truth*, *the ideal* and *the abstract*, is a bad metaphysician.

True metaphysic does not consist in making abstract what is perceptible, but in making perceptible what is abstract, apparent what is hidden, imaginable, if it may be, what is only intelligible, intelligible what withdraws itself from the attention.

Where spiritualism employs the words *God, creation, will, divine laws,* the materialist is perpetually obliged to make use of abstract terms, such as *nature, existence, effects.* He feeds his mind on ghosts without features, without color, without beauty.

Let us boldly affirm that oftentimes figurative expressions are the only ones that are fit to represent and make accurately conceivable the state of the soul and what passes within it, — that is to say, the truth. In vain would Hobbes banish them from argumentation: we must either retain them or deny ourselves many explanations. This is demanded not only by our understanding but by the nature of things. When the soul, holding intercourse with itself, presents to itself its own thoughts, it clothes them in figures and speaks to itself through images. This language is truly intimate. The language of the pure intellect, which the disciples of Malebranche have so much recommended, despoils thought of its pulp and of its colors, leaving only its dryest lineaments. This is the art of the neurologist or the geometrician. The soul does not thus restrict itself: it represents to itself the whole and depicts it fully; the pure intellect is only one of its aids.

Logic works; metaphysic contemplates.

Sophistry is a phantom, a semblance of good reasoning and of reason.

When, isolating the reasoning faculty from our other faculties, we succeed in rendering abstract, to the eyes of the mind, what in the world is most real and even most solid, both for the senses and for the heart, every thing is doubtful, every thing becomes problematical, and every thing may be contested. Why speak of order, of beauty? For the reasoning faculty isolated, there is nothing but *no* and *yes*, absences or existences, unities or nullities.

How many people make themselves abstract to appear profound! The greatest part of abstract terms are shadows that hide a vacuum.

In the mind there is a perpetual circulation of insensible reasonings.

To try a principle by its consequences is allowed by sound logic, and commanded by sound reason.

OF SYSTEMS, SPACE, AND TIME. 101

To combat objections, is often nothing more than to destroy phantoms; nothing is thereby cleared up; you only silence those who make things obscure.

Every system is an artifice, a fabrication, which interests me little; I examine what natural riches it contains, and regard only the treasure. Others, on the contrary, concern themselves only with the box; they know its dimensions, and whether it be of sandal-wood or aloes, of mahogany or of walnut. Silk-worms need, in order to spin, bits of wood placed in a certain manner; these must be left to them, supplied to them; it is not to the distaff that we should look, but to the silk.

Space is the stature of God.

Time is movement on space.

The year is a crown made of flowers, ears, fruits, and dry grass.

Light is, as it were, a divine humidity.

True and false diamonds have the same facets, the same transparency; but in the light of the former there is a light, a joy which is not found in the light of the latter; the true is wanting to them. Nothing is beautiful but the true.

The soul of the diamond is light.

Monuments are the grappling-irons that bind one generation to another. Preserve what your fathers have seen.

Agriculture produces good sense, and good sense of an excellent kind.

By gardening we enjoy the pure delicacies of agriculture.

What has God given to the wren? Content.

Rocks are the excuse and the ornament of sterility.

Carnivorous animals like not only the prey, but the chase. It is their play, their pastime, their pleasure.

The pleasure of the chase is the pleasure of attaining.

The odors of flowers are their souls.

When it rains, a certain obscurity makes all objects look extended. Moreover, by the disposition it obliges the body to make of itself, rain causes a kind of self-collectedness which renders the soul more impressible. The noise it makes, by occupying continuously the ear, awakens the attention and keeps it awake. . The kind of dull tint it gives to walls, to trees, to rocks, adds something to the impression caused by these objects. And, by obliging animals and men to be quiet and to keep under cover, it surrounds the traveller with a solitude and silence which complete the effect of making his sensations more distinct. Enveloped in his cloak, with his head covered, and walking in deserted paths, he is struck with every thing, and every thing is enlarged to his imagination or to his eyes. The brooks are swollen, the herbage is thicker, the minerals more apparent, the sky is nearer to the earth, and all objects, shut into a narrower horizon, seem to take up more room and to have more importance.

XII.

Of Governments and Constitutions; of Liberty, of Justice and the Laws; of Public and Private Morals, of the Character of Nations.

THE greatest need of a people is to be governed; its greatest happiness, to be well governed.*

The more moral force there is to oppose to physical force, the better constituted is the State.

The punishment of bad princes is to be thought worse than they are.

Every legitimate authority should love both its extent and its limitations.

Governments are things that establish themselves: they make themselves, they are not made. Strength is given them, support, consistency, but not being. Let us take it for certain that no gov-

---

* And no people ever will be perfectly well governed until it shall be entirely self-governed. The early training of Joubert, with the political anarchy and despotism of his later experience, rendered him incapable of valuing the latent innate capacity of men for religious, as well as for political, self-government.

ernment can be an affair of choice; it is almost always an affair of necessity.

Political constitutions have need of elasticity; they lose it when every thing is regulated by laws that are fixed and, so to speak, inflexible.

In political innovations every thing is done by compromise; and it is right that it should be.

One of the surest means of killing a tree is to uncover its roots. It is the same with institutions. We should not too much expose the origin of those we wish to preserve. All beginnings are small.

In all things let us be careful not to dig under the foundations.

In innovations there is nothing good but what is development, growth, completion.

Imitate time: it destroys every thing slowly; it undermines, it wears away, it detaches, it does not wrench.

To speak ever of prosperity and trade, is to speak like a merchant, and not like a philosopher. To aim but to enrich a people, is to act the banker, not the legislator.

Seek by means of science to render subsistence better, and thereby virtue easier, the soul more disposed to all that is good: that is the chief use of science.

Men are born unequal. The great benefit of society is to diminish this inequality so much as is possible, by procuring for all, security, property, education, and assistance.

How many shoulders without strength have asked for heavy burdens.

Never lift on high what is fragile.

The dregs may stir themselves as they please: they fall back to the bottom by their own coarseness.

Some men are only the valets of Providence; others are its ministers. The latter are they who, in executing its decrees, join their will with its will, their thought with its wisdom.

All great men have thought themselves more or less inspired.

The great men of certain times and certain circumstances are only men more stubbornly possessed than others with the opinion they all wish to make predominant.

All conquerors have had something common in their views, in their genius, and in their character.

Statesmen get drunk on the fumes of the wine they pour out, and their own falsehood deceives them.

Force and right rule all things in the world; force, before right arrives.

There is a right of the wisest, but not a right of the strongest.

Justice is truth in action.

Justice without strength, and strength without justice: fearful misfortunes!

It is in the order of things that a voluntary fault be followed by an inevitable pain.

Lenity is a part of justice; but she must not speak too loud, for fear of waking justice.

Formerly, it was thought, not that justice should spring from law, but law from justice.

The best laws grow out of usages.

The end, in history, is to appreciate men; in politics, to provide for the needs of the soul and the body; in morals, to perfect one's self; in literature, to delight and embellish the mind through the lights, the figures, and the colors of speech; in religion, to love Heaven; in all things, to know and improve every thing in one's self.

To ask for infallible, incorruptible human nature, is to ask for wind that has no mobility.

"I think as my fields think," said a landowner; a sentence full of meaning, the application of which we may make every day. Some, in short, think as their fields, others as their shop, others as their hammer, some others as their empty purse which aspires to get filled.

In the uneducated classes, the women are superior to the men; in the cultivated classes, on the contrary, we find the men superior to the women. It is because men are more susceptible of being rich in acquired virtues, and women in in-born virtues.

All luxury corrupts either the morals or the taste.

The idea of perfection is more necessary to men than models; I mean not merely in the arts, but also in morals.

It is not the desire for true riches that depraves man, but the desire for those that are false. A people never became corrupted for having grain, fruits, a pure air, better waters, more perfect arts, but for having gold, jewelry, subjects, power, a false renown, and an unjust superiority.

When you are told that a people is learned, inquire to what degree it knows the beautiful in Art.

Whatever grows corrupt, ferments.

In every age, even in the most enlightened, there is what may be justly called the spirit of the times, — a kind of atmosphere that will pass away, but which, while it lasts, deceives everybody as to the importance and even the truth of the dominant opinions.

Frenchmen are born volatile, but they are born moderate. They have a nimble mind that is agreeable, and not imposing. Among them, even sages, in their writings, seem to be young men.

No people in the world does wrong with so little

dignity as we. Our cupidity is marred by heedlessness, and our cunning by swagger. The moment we diverge from straightforwardness and generosity, we are ridiculous and displeasing, — our measures are narrow, our projects ill-concerted, our bearing even becomes that of a sharper. Other nations, more grave, more thoughtful, more deeply moved, soon make us their dupes, — they laugh and scoff at us as much as they like. Nothing becomes us but virtue; we exercise it with grace, and almost sportively; we do the noblest actions, and make the highest sacrifices, with ease, simplicity, grandeur; but we must be left to our instinct. If we are made to use means that are foreign to our nature, we become paltry, baffled intriguers, the playthings of everybody and worthy of contempt. Thence it is that the history of our armies is so rich, and that of our companies so poor. Look at the fate of our establishments in the Indies. We had it in our power, with the sword, to drive rival nations from a post which they occupied, and by our temper to make for ourselves more friends than they in those countries. America and India cannot charge us with blood unjustly shed, and we have no cause to dread either their vengeance or their hatred; but we have often had to blush for their just disdain of us; we never knew how to supplant those other nations in commerce; and often they have driven away our agents with ignominy, as blundering rogues, — impudent enough to try to be cheats, but without skill or aptitude. Bad faith has need of combinations, precautions, secrecy, slowness: the Frenchman is not adapted to it. He only succeeds well in feelings that require dash; and in commerce that needs taste, boldness, and celerity.

In France, it seems, we love the Arts more to judge of them than to enjoy them.

For French heads, you must arrange the wind, and choose it, for all winds make them turn.

We have still in France an expression which is a remnant and a sign of the nobleness and disinterestedness that were formerly common. In our small towns, they say of a man who loves to hoard, "He clings to matter," — a most philosophical expression, and which assuredly does honor to the nation with whom it is in use.

The wisdom of Bonaparte was in his thoughts, his folly in his passions.

In England, the Parliament is king, and the king is minister, — but an hereditary, perpetual, inviolable minister. He is a mutilated monarch, with one eye, one leg, and one arm, but honored.

Englishmen are honest in private affairs, and dishonest in national.

Englishmen are brought up to respect serious things, and Frenchmen to laugh at them.

Fox was a man who, in all the acceptations of our French word, knew how to make an appearance (*se montrer*); and he knew nothing else.

Pride is the dominant characteristic of the Spanish people. Even in their passion for gold there is more pride than cupidity. It is the lustre of this metal, its purity, its grandeur, and, so to speak, its glory, that make it so dear to the Spaniard. He looks upon it as the king of metals, and thinks himself, as being of the noblest nation on earth, alone worthy to possess it. Thence he was pitiless toward the Indians, to wrest from them this sovereign substance, which, in the hands of a naked people, seemed to him a captive.

Frederick II., this king without women, will never be my hero. His famous tactics were shown to be unworthy of their renown, when they undertook, in these latter times, to measure themselves with our French impetuosity. These so much vaunted Prussians were always beaten before they had got into line, while they were still in the midst of their long evolutions. If his military institutions have already proved a failure, how will it be with his moral, or, rather, with his influence of all kinds which planted in the Prussian mind so much indifference for every thing that is grave and serious, except labor and war? He made his country richer, more warlike; he did not make it better.

Politeness in manners, and barbarism in morals; weakness, through ignorance; and presumption, through success; natural imperfection, and borrowed excellence; vices that are a thousand years old, and will be eternal, because they are in the race, the tendencies, and the climate; virtues that will be short-lived, because they are artificial and not in the blood; a people, in short, of which has been made what it cannot be, and which is doomed to re-become what it was: such are the Russians.

This is the way that commerce might be distributed among nations, according to their characters: the Spaniard — jeweler, goldsmith, lapidary; the Englishman — manufacturer; the German — paper-dealer; the Hollander — vender of comestibles; and the Frenchman — a milliner. In navigation, the first is courageous; the second, skilful; the third, learned; the fourth, industrious; and the fifth, adventurous. A vessel should have a Spanish captain, an English pilot, a German mate, and Holland sailors; the Frenchman only goes on his own account. To the first you must propose a conquest; an undertaking, to the second; researches, to the third; to the fourth, gain; and a *coup de main*, to the fifth. The first would like vast voyages; the second, important voyages; the third, useful ones; the fourth, lucrative ones; and the fifth, quick voyages. The first embarks in order to go; the second, to act; the third, to see; the fourth, to gain; and the fifth, to arrive. The sea, in short, is, for the Spaniard, a road; for the Englishman, a place; for the German, a study; for the Hollander, a means of transportation; and for the Frenchman, a post-chaise.

XIII.

OF ANTIQUITY; OF THE AGE.

THREE things attached the ancients to their native soil: temples, tombs, and ancestors. The two great ties that bound them to their government were custom and antiquity. With the moderns, hope and love of novelty have changed every thing. The ancients said *our ancestors;* we say *posterity.* We do not love, as they did, our country, — that is, the land and laws of our fathers; we love rather the land and laws of our children; it is the magic of the future, and not that of the past, that charms us.

Many words have changed meaning. The word *liberty*, for example, had, at bottom, with the ancients, the same meaning as that of *dominium.* "I wish to be free," meant, with them, "I wish to govern or administer the city:" and means, with us, "I wish to be independent." *Liberty*, with us, has a moral meaning; with them, it had a meaning wholly political.

The ancients, whom every thing in their institutions materialized, were spiritualized by their poetry. They said there was a Muse who presided over the science of government.

At the foot of the altars of their gods, in addressing to them agreeable and gentle words, the ancients learned to be gentle, cultivated, polite in their speech with men. They made this prayer to Venus: "Grant us to say nothing but what is agreeable, and to do nothing but what shall please!"

Athenian politeness was superior to ours. It had almost the language of gallantry. Socrates, in the banquet of Plato, says to Alcibiades: "The eyes of the spirit become more piercing at the age when the eyes of the body grow weak, and you are yet far from that age." What grace in the contradiction!

One day some one asked the daughter of Aristotle, named Pythias, what color pleased her most. She answered, that which arose from modesty on the countenance of a man who is simple and kindly.

The mind of the Athenians was naturally noble and pathetic, as that of the French is naturally agreeable.

Contempt for private insult was one of the characteristics of ancient morals.

With the Greeks, and above all with the Athenians, the beautiful was the literary and civil; with the Romans, the moral and political; with the Jews, the religious and domestic beautiful; with other peoples, the imitation of these three.

It seems to me much more difficult to be a modern than to be an ancient.

When I speak of antiquity, I mean healthy antiquity; for there was a distempered and frenzied antiquity, — that of Porphyry and of Jamblichus.

Even the dregs of Greek literature, in its old age, offers a delicate residuum.

The ancients should be read slowly; much patience, that is, much attention, is needed, in order to have much pleasure, when we peruse beautiful works.

Antiquity! I like its ruins better than its reconstructions.

The ancients had in their mind much less movement and more dignity than we have. Thence the moderation of their speech and the excellence of their taste.

Civilization! A great word much abused, and whose proper meaning is what renders civil. There is then civilization through religion, modesty, benevolence, justice, — for all these unite men; and incivilization, or return to barbarism, through the spirit of disputation, through irreligion, impudence, audacity, ambition of all, constant love of one's comfort, greed of gain, — for all these sever men and attach us but to ourselves.

When I see young people such as those of our day, I think that Heaven wishes to destroy the world.

Why are we so sensible to impressions from things agreeable or painful? Our fathers were less so. It is because our minds are more empty and our weakness greater. We are less occupied with serious feelings or solid thoughts. The man who has only his duty in view, and who pursues it steadily, pays less attention to what is on his road.

Minds fit to govern not only great States, but even their own house, are hardly ever met with nowadays. At no period were they so rare.

There are no longer irreconcilable enmities, because there are no disinterested sentiments; it is a good born of an evil.

Nowadays we have not only the desire, but the ambition, of gain.

The same spirit of revolution has governed men in literature, in the state, and in religion. The philosophers have wished to substitute their books for the Bible, as the Jacobins their authority for that of the king.

The age is afflicted with the most fearful of mental maladies, — the disgust of religion. It is not religious liberty that is demanded, but irreligious liberty.*

They have broken up the roads that lead to heaven, and which all the world followed; we must now make ourselves ladders.

We live in such extraordinary conjunctures that the aged have no more experience of them than the young. We are all novices, because every thing is new.

* In reading thoughts like this and the following, and some others, the reader should bear in mind that they were written at the end of the last century or at the beginning of this, in France, by a man of a deeply religious nature, and a devout Catholic.

To be capable of respect is, in these days, almost as rare as to be worthy of it.

The age thought it was making progress in going over precipices.

In literature, nothing makes a mind so imprudent and so impudent as ignorance of past times and contempt for ancient books.

Our fathers judged of books with their taste, their conscience, and their reason; we judge of them by the emotions that they cause. "Will this book do good or harm? is it calculated to improve or to corrupt the mind?" — great questions which our predecessors asked themselves. We ask, "Will it give pleasure?"

There was a time when the world acted upon books. Now books act upon the world.

French authors think, write, speak, judge, and imagine too fast. And this comes from a radical vice of our habits, — we are too much in a hurry to live and to enjoy.

We don't write our books after they are made, but we make them while writing them. Thence the best that is in them is masked by scaffoldings.

They are full of what ought to be put in, and what ought to be left out.

In books, I see everywhere will, but not intellect. Ideas! Who has ideas? There are plenty of approvals and disapprovals; the mind gives its consents or its denials; it judges, but it does not see.

Almost everybody in these days excels in refinements of style; it is an art that has become common. The exquisite is everywhere; the satisfactory, nowhere. "I should like to smell manure," said a woman of wit!

It is indescribable to what degree literature has grown sensual. In the austerest works there must be something enticing, something alluring. What pleases is confounded with what is beautiful.

You find, almost everywhere, nothing but words that are clear, and thoughts that are not so.

XIV.

OF EDUCATION; OF THE FINE ARTS; OF POETRY; OF STYLE.

THE idea of order in all things — that is to say, literary, moral, political, and religious order, is the basis of all education.

Children have more need of models than of critics.

Education should be tender and severe, and not cold and soft.

Man might be so educated that all his prepossessions would be truths, and all his feelings virtues.

Young girls should be put to work on nothing that is too terrestrial and too material. Only light objects should go into their hands. Whatever fully exercises the sense of touch, especially on living things, is unsuited to their purity and would destroy it. Of this they have so strong an instinct that they look much and touch little, — even the most delicate things they touch only with the tips of their fingers. They are like the imagination, and should only skim along the surface, as that does. Among our senses, the least virginal is that of touch. Observe also that a girl does not touch as a woman does, nor a woman chaste in soul as one who is not so.

In bringing up a child, think of its old age.

To every one should be left his measure of intellect, his character, and his temperament, contenting ourselves with improving and making the most of them. Nothing so becomes the mind as its natural carriage ; hence its ease, its grace, and all its real or apparent facilities. Whatever strains it, hurts it; to force its springs, is to ruin it. We all bear some marks of our destination. These should not be effaced, but followed ; otherwise, we shall be sure to have a false and unhappy career. Those who are born delicate should live delicately, but healthily ; those who are born robust should live robustly, but temperately ; those who have a quick mind let them keep their wings, and let the others keep their feet.

It is not sufficiently noted to what degree the manners and moods of the teacher, exhibited in his countenance, have an influence on children and form or deform them.

A mild light, imperceptibly insinuated into the mind of the young, carries thither a joy which increases with reflection.

The object of Art is to unite matter to forms; and forms are that which Nature has most true, most beautiful, and most pure.

Far from relegating the Fine Arts to the class of useful superfluities, they should be accounted among the most precious and most important possessions of human society. Without them sublime minds could not make known to us the greatest part of their conceptions. Without the Fine Arts the most perfect and most just man could only experience a part of the enjoyments of which his excellence makes him susceptible, and of the happiness that Nature designed for him. There are emotions so delicate and objects so enchanting that it were impossible to express them except with colors or with sounds. The Arts should be looked upon as a kind of language apart — as a unique means of communication between the inhabitants of a superior sphere and ourselves.

In all the Arts the most beautiful expressions are those that seem born of a high contemplation.

The intellect should produce effects similar to

itself,—that is to say, sentiments and ideas; and the Arts should aim at the effects of the intellect. Artist! if thou causest only sensations, what dost thou with thy art, that a prostitute with her trade and the executioner with his cannot do as well as thou ? If there is only body in thy work, and that it speaks but to the senses, thou art but a workman without soul, and all thy skill is in thy hands!

The beautiful!—it is beauty seen with the eyes of the soul.

The ordinary true, or purely real, cannot be the object of the Arts. Illusion on a ground of truth — that is the secret of the Fine Arts.

In Art there are many beauties that become natural only by dint of art.

Sculptors and painters show us scarcely any thing but bodies uninhabited. The painter and sculptor who does not know how to make visible in his figures the immateriality and immortality of the soul, produces nothing that is truly beautiful.

Funereal music seems to let the sounds die.

What is poetry? At this moment, I cannot say; but I maintain that in words used by the true poet there is found for the eyes a certain phosphorus, for the taste a certain nectar, for the attention an ambrosia, not found in them when used by any one else.

The inarticulate utterances of the passions are not more natural to man than poetry.

The intellect has no share in genuine poetry, which is a gift of Heaven; it springs only out of the soul; it comes in reverie; but, do what we will, reflection never finds it. The intellect, however, prepares it by offering to the soul objects which reflection, in a measure, unearths. Emotion and knowledge,—here is its cause, and here its subject.

Poets are children with much grandeur of soul and with a celestial intelligence.

It is, above all, in the spirituality of ideas that poetry consists.

High poetry is chaste and pious by its essence—let us even say by position; for its natural place keeps it raised above the earth and makes it a neighbor of Heaven. From this elevation, like the immortal spirits, it sees souls, thoughts, and bodies but little.

Nature well-ordered — contemplated by man well-ordered — is the basis, the substance, the essence of the poetic.

Poets have a hundred times more good sense than philosophers. In seeking the beautiful, they find more truths than philosophers do in seeking the true.

Poets who, in epic poetry, represent a communication perpetually open between the earth and heaven, and maintained by beings intermediary between men and gods, have only imagined and confusedly depicted the true state of the world as to what is most worthy to be known and most hidden from our eyes.

The true poet has words that show his thought, thoughts that let you see into his soul, and a soul where every thing is painted distinctly. He has a mind full of very clear images, while ours is only filled with confused descriptions.

Poets are more inspired by the images than by the presence of objects.

To be good and to be a poet, we must first clothe what we look upon and see nothing quite naked. We must, at least, put our good-will and a certain amenity between all objects and ourselves.

It is not enough that a poem have poetry of images; it must have also poetry of ideas.

Beautiful verses are exhaled like sounds or perfumes.

There are verses which, by their character, seem to belong to the mineral kingdom: they have ductility and lustre; others to the vegetable kingdom: they have sap; others, finally, to the animated kingdom: and they have life. The most beautiful are those that have soul; they belong to the three kingdoms, but to the Muse still more.

Beautiful poems, epic, dramatic, lyric, are nothing else than the waking dreams of a sage.

The poet should not traverse at a walk an interval which he can clear at a bound.

In the poetic style every word resounds like the twang of a lyre well strung, and leaves after it a number of undulations.

His subject should offer to the genius of the

OF POETRY.   129

poet a kind of fanciful domain, which he can expand and contract at will. A place too real, personages too historical, imprison the mind and cramp its movements.

An epic or didactic poem that cannot be read in a day, is too long.

You will find poetry nowhere unless you bring some with you.

Words become luminous when the finger of the poet touches them with his phosphorus.

In order that words be poetical they should be warm with the fire of the soul, or moist with its breath.

Like the nectar of the bee, which turns to honey the dust of flowers, or like that liquor which converts lead into gold, the poet has a breath that fills out words, makes them light, and colors them. He knows wherein consists the charm of words, and by what art enchanted piles may be built with them.

To fill an old word with a new meaning, of which usage or age had emptied it, so to speak, this is not to innovate, it is to rejuvenate. We enrich languages by digging into them. They should be treated like fields: to make them fertile when they are no longer young, they must be stirred at great depths.

All languages abound in gold.

To restore to words their physical primitive meaning is to furbish them, to clean them, to give them back their first brightness; it is to remelt this coin and return it to circulation more glittering; it is to renew the worn out impress.

Old books are good to read; through them we go back to the sources of a language and survey it in its whole course. To write French well, we should understand Gallic. Our language is like a mine in which gold is only found at certain depths.

Before using a beautiful word, make a place for it.

In order that an expression be beautiful, it must say more than is necessary; saying it, however, with precision; it must have in it abundance and economy; the *narrow* and the *vast*, the *little* and the *much* must meet in it; in short, it must have a brief sound and an infinite meaning. Whatever is luminous has this character. A lamp lights up the object for which it is used, and at the same time twenty objects one has no thought of.

There is harmony for the mind whenever there is perfect propriety in the expressions. Now, when the mind is satisfied, it takes no heed of what the ear desires.

It is not so much the sound as the meaning of words that so often holds in suspense the pen of good writers. Well-chosen words are abridged sentences.

It were strange, should it turn out, that style is only beautiful when it has some obscurity, that is to say, some clouds; and perhaps this is true when the obscurity comes from its very excellence, from choosing words that are not common, from choosing words that are not vulgar. Certain it is, that in the beautiful there is always visible beauty and hidden beauty. It is, moreover, certain that it has never so many charms for us as when we read it attentively in a language which we only half understand.

Sometimes the vague word is preferable to the accurate. According to the phrase of Boileau, there are obscurities that are elegant, some that are majestic, some even that are necessary; they are those that make the mind imagine what it would not be possible for clearness to make it see.

Take from words all indefiniteness, and make of them invariable signs, there will be no more play in speech, and thence no more eloquence, no more poetry. All that is changeful and mobile in the affections of the soul will remain without possible expression. I say more: if you banish all abuse in words, you will have no more axioms even. It is the ambiguity, the uncertainty, — that is to say, the suppleness of words, which is one of their great advantages, and which enables us to make an exact use of them.

Let not the word clasp the thought too closely; let it be for it a body which does not compress it; nothing too tight-fitting — grand rule for grace, in literary work and in manners.

Words are never wanting to ideas; it is ideas that are wanting to words. So soon as the idea is come to its last degree of perfection, the word is born, presents itself, and clothes it.

When we are satisfied with half understanding, we are satisfied with half expressing, and then we write with ease.

The best literary periods have always been those when authors weighed and counted their words.

"Style," says Dussault, "is a habit of the mind." Happy they in whom it is a habit of the soul.

With some, style grows out of thoughts; with others, thoughts grow out of style.

Keep your mind above your thoughts, and your thoughts above your expressions.

Thoughts should be born of the soul, words of thoughts, and sentences of words.

It is with our thoughts as with our flowers, — those that are simple in expression carry their seed with them; those that are double through richness and pomp charm the mind, but produce nothing.

Literary style consists in giving a body and a shape to thought by means of the sentence.

Attention has a narrow mouth; we must pour into it what we say with care, and, as it were, drop by drop.

The temperate style is the only classical one.

It is a great art that of knowing how to point one's thought and thrust it into the attention.

Graceful conciseness, unique beauty of style.

Beware of the tricks of style.

The true character of epistolary style is playfulness and urbanity.

XV.

OF THE QUALITIES OF THE WRITER, AND OF LITERARY COMPOSITIONS.

OF literary qualities, some come from the organization, others from the soul; some from culture, others from nature. Animation, for example, is given to us, and good taste is acquired. Insight is of the soul, and skill comes from practice. But what comes from the soul is more beautiful, and what is natural to us is more divine.

To produce a fine work it is not enough to be clear and to be understood; you must please, you must fascinate and put illusions into all eyes; I mean those illusions that give light, not those that deceive by distorting objects. Now, to please and to fascinate, we want something besides the truth; we must have the man; the thought and emotion peculiar to him who speaks must be felt. It is human warmth and almost human substance which gives to all things that quality which charms us.

There must be enthusiasm in the voice, to be a

great singer ; in color, to be a great painter ; in sounds, to be a great musician ; and in words, to be a great writer. But this enthusiasm must be concealed and almost imperceptible: this it is that makes the spell.

Without transport or, rather, without rapture of mind, no genius.

Our ideas, like pictures, are made up of lights and shadows.

There are two kinds of genius ; the one seizes at a glance what concerns human life ; the other, what concerns things divine, souls. One can hardly have the first fully and perfectly without having also some portion of the second ; but one may have the second without the first, for things human depend on things divine and touch them on all sides without their being reciprocity. Heaven could subsist without the earth, not the earth without heaven.

There is one kind of genius which seems to hold of the earth : that is force ; another kind which holds of the earth and heaven : that is elevation ; and, finally, another which holds of God : that is light and wisdom, or the light of the mind. All light comes from above.

Mind ruling matter, reason taming the passions, and taste mastering excitement, are the characteristics of the beautiful.

Wisdom is the beginning of the beautiful.

The water that falls from heaven is more fertile.

The sublime is the summit of the great.

Where there is no refinement, there is no literature.

Books, thoughts, and style that are sober have on the mind the good effect that a calm countenance has on our eyes and our temper.

An imagination chastened and wise is the only merit that can give a book value.

Words, writings, poetry in which there is more repose, but a repose that moves us, are more beautiful than those in which there is more movement. The movement given by the motionless is the most perfect and the most delightful; it is like that which God impresses on the world; so that the writer who causes it produces an effect that has in it something divine.

Splendor is a lustre that is calm, interior, uniform at all points; brilliancy, a lustre that does not prevail in the whole mass, does not penetrate it, and is only met with in places.

Genuine depth comes from concentrated ideas.

Certain authors are blamed for a too-labored study in style. For myself, I like to find in books the right expression, the simple expression, the expression the most suitable to the subject treated, to the thought one has, to the feeling with which one is animated, to what precedes and to what follows, to the place the word is to fill. People speak of naturalness; but there is a coarse naturalness and a refined naturalness. The natural expression is not always that which is most in use, but that which suits the essential nature of what is to be expressed. Custom is not nature, and the best is not what comes first, but what is to remain always.

In some performances the voices of women are heard rather than those of men. The voice of wisdom is between the two, like a celestial voice, which is of no sex. Such is that of Fenelon and of Plato.

Naturalness! Art must work it up — must spin and polish this silk.

He who writes with ease always thinks that he has more talent than he really has. To write well, there is needed a natural facility with an acquired difficulty.

Facility is opposed to the sublime. Look at Cicero: he wants nothing but the obstacle and the leap.

Sagacity needs but a moment to perceive; precision needs years to express.

Genius begins beautiful works, but only labor finishes them.

Ignorance, which in morals extenuates a fault, is itself, in literature, a cardinal fault.

It is only a long time after having learnt it that we know any thing well.

This were perhaps not an unimportant advice to give to writers: never write any thing that does not give you great enjoyment; emotion is easily propagated from the writer to the reader.

We should avoid, in all literary work, whatever separates the intellect from the soul. The habit of abstract reasoning has this terrible drawback.

Young writers give their minds much exercise and little food.

To make that agreeable which was never so before is a kind of creation.

Commonplaces have an everlasting interest. It is the uniform stuff which, always and everywhere, the human mind must work up when it wishes to please. Circumstances throw their variety into them. No music is more agreeable than variations of known airs.

He who does all that he can exposes himself to the danger of showing his limits. We should push to the extreme neither our talent, our strength, nor our expenditure.

A work of art should have the air, not of a reality, but of an idea. Our ideas are always at once more noble, more beautiful, more adapted to touch the soul than the objects they represent, even when well represented.

The thoughts that come to us have more value than those we get by seeking. They start up under our feet, in the path of life, like those springs that burst forth under our tread without our thinking of them.

The fine feelings and ideas that we wish to set forth in our writings should be very familiar to us, in order that the charm of intimacy be felt in their expression.

We should describe objects only to describe the feelings they occasion, for speech should at once represent the thing and the author, the subject and the thought. All that we say should be dyed with ourselves, with our soul. This operation is long, but it immortalizes every thing.

The mind conceives with pain, but it brings forth with delight.

To make a good book three things are necessary: talent, art, and avocation — that is to say: nature, industry, and practice.

When writing, we should recollect that scholars are there; but it is not to them that we should address ourselves.

For an ordinary book all that is wanted is a subject, but for a fine work there is wanted a germ which develops itself in the mind like a plant. The only beautiful works are those that have been for a long while, if not worked on, at least thought upon.

Literary and poetic order is in the natural and free succession of movements. The beautiful disorder of which Boileau speaks is an apparent disorder and a real order.

In the *lucidus ordo* of Horace, there is something siderial. Our dry method is rather an *ordo ligneus vel ferreus* (a wooden or iron order); the parts are all riveted or mortised together.

The best thoughts of certain writers seem to me to have taken up no more room in their mind than they occupy on their paper. In their ideas I see only luminous points surrounded by obscurity. There is nothing in them that reëchoes, nothing that freely moves in a space larger than itself.

It is only his thoughts, and they taken separately, that characterize a writer. Rightly are they called characteristics, and are cited; they show the head and face, so to speak; the rest only shows the hands.

There come into the head many useless phrases, but the mind grinds its colors out of them.

All eloquence should come from emotion, and all emotion naturally gives eloquence.

In the mind of certain writers nothing is grouped, or draped, or modelled; their pages present a flat surface on which roll words.

In composing, we do not perfectly know what we wished to say until it is said. It is, in fact, the word that finishes the idea and gives it existence.

The end of a work should always make us remember the beginning.

The reason why we seek long in composing or creating is, that we do not seek where we should, and that we seek where we should not. Happily, in thus straying, we make discoveries, we have fortunate encounters, and are often indemnified for what we seek without finding it by what we find without seeking it.

The orator is occupied with his subject, and the declaimer with his part — the one is in earnest, the other feigns; the first is a man unfolding large ideas, and the second a person delivering himself of big words.

With historic recitals should be mingled only such reflections as the intelligence of a judicious reader would not suffice to suggest to him.

There is a great charm in seeing facts through words, because then we see them through thoughts.

The comic grows out of a serious ground; the pathetic out of the patience or repose of him who suffers. Thence, there is no comic without gravity, and no pathetic without moderation. He who makes us laugh should forget that he is doing so, and he who makes us weep should withhold his tears.

Alas! in order to please a corrupted people, you must describe passions that are, like themselves, ungoverned. Souls, to whom their own licentiousness has made strong sensations necessary, are, in their insatiable hunger, greedy of excess. It is thus that men accustomed to the fear of the tempest, to the hope of calm, to all the great movements that attend long and perilous voyages, have no longer a taste for the repose of the land and yearn for the sea and its dangers, the storm and its terrors.

There never was a literary age whose dominant taste was not sickly. The success of excellent authors consists in making wholesome works agreeable to morbid tastes.

A sound taste is one that knows how to distinguish between matter and form, and to separate defects of form from excellence of substance, defects of substance from excellence of form.

Where are not agreeableness and some serenity, there we have no *belles-lettres*.

Criticism is a methodical exercise of discernment.

Professional critics are incapable of distinguishing and appreciating either diamonds in the rough state or gold in bars. They are traders, and in literature know only the coins that are current. Their criticism has scales and weights, but neither crucible nor touchstone.

Certain critics are much like people who, when they laugh, exhibit ugly teeth.

Taste is the literary conscience of the soul.

Good judgment in literature is a faculty of very slow growth, which only at a late period reaches its last point of growth.

When in a nation an individual is born capable of producing a great thought, another is born capable of comprehending it and of admiring it.

Writers of influence are only men who express well what others think, and who awaken in minds sentiments and ideas which were ready to be awakened. Literatures lie at the bottom of the general mind.

Memory loves only what is excellent.

What astonishes astonishes once, but what is admirable is more and more admired.

From the first sight of it, perfection leaves nothing to desire, but it ever leaves some beauty, some charm, some merit to be discovered.

Beautiful works do not intoxicate, but they enchant.

From all well-wrought works there results a kind of incorporeal form which fixes itself easily in the memory.

It is not the opinions of authors and that part of their teachings, which may be called assertions, that do the most to instruct and nourish the mind. In great writers there is a concealed and invisible juice that is imbibed in the reading of them — an indescribable, inassignable fluid — a salt, a subtle principle more nutritive than all the rest.

There are books from which one inhales an exquisite air.

Between esteem and contempt, there is in literature a road all bordered with success without glory, which is also obtained without merit.

Talent betakes itself to where is heard the voice of praise. Praise is the syren that leads it astray.

How many books there are whose reputation is made that would not obtain it were it now to make.

To mediocre people the mediocre is the excellent.

By nature the mind abstains from judging what it does not know. It is vanity that forces it to speak when it would prefer to be silent.

The bee and the wasp suck the same flowers, but both do not know how to find in them the same honey.

In the majority of agreeable books there is nothing but a prattle that does not tire you.

Nothing is worse than a mediocre work that makes a pretension to be excellent.

With some, to write is their occupation, their business, their life; with others, their amusement, their distraction, their play. With the former it is magistracy, function, duty, inspiration; with the latter, task, trade, calculation, deliberate purpose. The former write to diffuse what they deem better for all; the latter, to display what they think better for themselves. The first wish to do what is right; the others, what is expedient; proposing to themselves for end, — the first, truth; the others, profit.

True men of science and true poets become such by enjoyment more than by labor. What precipitates them into their studies, and then keeps them there, is not their ambition, but their genius.

The products of certain minds come, not from their soil, but from the manure wherewith it has been covered.

It is a hundred times better to adapt a work to the nature of the human mind than to what is called the state of society. In man there is something immutable; thence it is that in the arts and in works of art there are unchangeable rules — beauties that will always please, or contrivances that will please but for a short time.

The literature of nations begins with fables and ends with romances.

Books give us some of our highest pleasures, and men our deepest pains. Sometimes, even thoughts console us for things, and books for men.

Nothing is more beautiful than a beautiful book.

Profuseness of words and thoughts betrays an extravagant mind. It is not abundance, but excellence that constitutes wealth. Economy in literature announces the superior writer. Without good order and sobriety, no wisdom; without wisdom, no grandeur.

Beware of expanding what is clear. These useless explanations, these too continuous statements, present the uniform whiteness of a long wall and cause us the same weariness. A man is not an architect because he has built an immense wall, nor has one accomplished a literary work because he has written a huge book. To write a book or write a work are two things. A literary work is produced by means of art, a book by means of ink and paper. You may produce a work in two pages, and only make a book although you fill ten volumes *folio*.

The extent of a palace is measured from east to west, or from north to south; but that of a literary work, from the earth to heaven; so that there may be found as much range and power of mind in a few pages — in an ode, for example — as in a whole epic poem.

A few words worthy to be remembered suffice to give an idea of a great mind. There are single thoughts that contain the essence of a whole volume, single sentences that have the beauties of a large work, a simplicity so finished and so perfect that it equals in merit and in excellence a large and glorious composition.

What is exquisite is worth more than what is ample. Dealers have great respect for big books, but readers prefer small ones — they last longer and go farther. Virgil and Horace have but one volume. Homer, Æschylus, Sophocles, Euripides, and Terence have not more. Menander, who delights us, is reduced to a few leaves. Without Telemachus, who would know Fenelon? Who would know Bossuet without his *Funeral Orations* and his *Discourse on Universal History?* Pascal, la Bruyere, Vauvenargues, and la Rochefoucault, Boileau, Racine, and la Fontaine occupy but little space, and are the delight of the refined. Very good writers write little, because they need much time to reduce to beauty their abundance and wealth.

Remember what St. Francis of Sales said, in speaking of the *Imitation of Jesus Christ*, — " I have sought repose everywhere, and have only found it in a little corner, with a little book." Happy is the writer who can make a beautiful little book!

XVI.

LITERARY JUDGMENTS.

THERE never will be an endurable translation of Homer, until all the words be chosen with art, and be full of variety, of novelty and grace. The diction, moreover, must be as antique, as plain as the manners, the events, and the personages described. With our modern style, every thing is distorted in Homer, and his heroes seem grotesque figures that play the grave and the proud.

Plato found philosophy made of bricks, and made it of gold.

I admire in Plato that eloquence which dispenses with all the passions, and needs them not for its triumph. That is the characteristic of this great metaphysician.

In Plato there is a light ever about to show itself and which never does. It is seen in his veins as in those of the flint, and his thoughts have but to be struck to make it flash. He piles up clouds; but they contain a celestial fire, which only awaits the shock.

With a mind, in its nature, of flame, not merely illuminated, but luminous, Plato shines with his own light. It is the splendor of his thought that dyes his language. In him lustre is born of sublimity.

From the writings of Plato there rises what may be termed an intellectual vapor.

In Plato seek only forms and ideas: these are what he himself sought. There is in him more light than objects, more form than substance. He should be inhaled, not fed on.

Plato shows us nothing, but he puts light into our eyes, and causes in us a brilliancy wherewith all objects become afterward illuminated. He teaches us nothing, but he disciplines us, shapes us, and makes us apprehensive. The study of him, one knows not how, increases in us the susceptibility to distinguish and to accept all beautiful truths that may present themselves. Like mountain-air, it sharpens the appetite, and gives a taste for wholesome food.

Circuities, when they are not necessary, and

explanations of what is clear, are the defects of Plato. Like children, he troubles clear water for the pleasure of seeing it settle and clarify. This indeed he does, the better to exhibit the character of the personage in hand; but he thus sacrifices the piece to the actor, the fable to the mask.

In Plato, the spirit of poetry gives life to the languor of dialectics.

Plato loses himself in the void; but we see the play of his wings and hear their rustle.

Socrates, in Plato, shows himself too often a philosopher by profession, instead of being content to be one by nature and by virtue.

Aristotle put the dialogues of Plato into the class of epic poetry. He was right; and Marmontel, who contradicts him, did not know the nature and character of these dialogues, and did not understand Aristotle.

Aristotle rectified all the rules, and in all the sciences added new truths to known truths. His works are an ocean of learning, an encyclopedia of antiquity.

The *Memorabilia* of Xenophon are a fine thread

with which he has the art of making magnificent lace, but with which we can sew nothing.

Cicero is, in philosophy, a kind of moon. His doctrine has a light that is very soft, but borrowed, a light purely Greek, which the Roman softened and weakened.

There are a thousand ways of preparing and seasoning words; Cicero loved them all.

In Catullus are found two things, than the union of which nothing can be worse; affected delicacy and grossness.

It is the symmetries of the style of Seneca that make him quoted.

Take from Juvenal his gall, and from Virgil his wisdom, and you have two bad writers.

I look upon *Plutarch's Lives* as one of the most precious monuments bequeathed to us by antiquity. There we are shown whatever has appeared that is great* in human kind, and the best that men have done is held before us as an example. All ancient wisdom is there. For the writer

* Joubert means, of course, in ancient Greece and ancient Rome.

I have not the same esteem that I have for his compilation. Commendable for many virtues, he who would not allow his old slaves to be sold nor the animals that work or accident had mutilated in his service, he is not commendable for the pusillanimity that lets him fluctuate among the opinions of philosophers, without having the courage to contradict or to back them, and which makes him entertain for all men of celebrity the respect that is only due to those who were virtuous or just. He throws a soft light even upon crimes.

Pliny the younger was very particular about his words, but not so about his thoughts.

Plutarch, in interpreting Plato, is clearer than he is, and nevertheless he has less light and causes to the soul less joy.

In the annals of Tacitus, there is a narrative interest which will not permit us to read little, and a depth and grandeur of expression which will not permit us to read much. The mind, divided between the curiosity that hurries it along, and the attention which makes it pause, experiences some fatigue : the writer takes possession of the reader even to doing him violence.

The style of St. Jerome shines like ebony.

The style of Tacitus was fitted to paint dark souls and disastrous times.

St. Thomas and St. Augustin are the Aristotle and the Plato of theology. But St. Thomas is more an Aristotle than St. Augustin is a Plato.

The greater part of the thoughts of Pascal on laws, usages, customs, are but the thoughts of Montaigne recast.

Behind the thought of Pascal is discerned the attitude of a mind that is steadfast, and free from all passion. It is that especially which makes him so imposing.

In the style of Bossuet Gallic freedom and kindliness make themselves felt with grandeur. He is stately and sublime, popular and almost naïve.

Fenelon dwells amid the valleys and slopes of thought; Bossuet on its heights and summits.

M. de Beausset says of Fenelon: "He loved men more than he knew them." This is charming: it were impossible to praise with more wit what one blames, or to praise more highly while blaming.

As Plato had carried his imagination into metaphysics, Bacon carried his into physics, as bold and adventurous in establishing conjectures, in invoking experience, as Plato was magnificent in setting forth likelihoods. Plato, at least, gives his ideas for ideas; but Bacon gives his for facts. Thence he misleads more in physics than Plato does in metaphysics. Look at his *History of Life and Death*. Both, however, were great and splendid minds. Both opened grand roads into the domains of literature; Bacon with a light firm foot, Plato with wide wings.

Locke almost always proves himself an ingenious logician, but a bad metaphysician, an antimetaphysician. He was, indeed, not only destitute of metaphysics: he was incapable of and an enemy of them. A good interrogator, a good groper, but without light, he is a blind man who makes good use of his stick.

Voltaire retained through life, in the world and in business, a very strong impress from the influence of his first masters. Impetuous as a poet, and polite as a courtier, he knows how to be as insinuating and crafty as a Jesuit. No one ever followed more carefully, and with more art and shrewdness, the famous maxim he so much ridiculed: *To be all things to all men.* With him the desire to please was even stronger than the desire to rule, and he had more satisfaction in bringing into play his seductions than his strength. He took especial pains to win men of letters, and treated as enemies only those whom he had not been able to gain over.

Voltaire is sometimes sad; he is excited; but he is never serious. His graces even are impudent.

There are defects difficult to perceive, that have not been classed, or defined, and have no names. Voltaire is full of them.

Voltaire, in his writings, is never alone with himself. Perpetual gazeteer, every day he kept the public informed of the events of yesterday. His temper and mood did him more service in writing than his reason or his knowledge. Some individual hatred or contempt was the moving cause of all his works. Even his tragedies are only the satire of some opinion.

Voltaire's is the most licentious of minds, and, what is worse, his readers grow infected with his spirit. Sobriety, in restraining his humors, would certainly have deprived him of half his power. His mind, in order to play freely, had need of license. And yet, never was there a man less independent. Sad condition, deplorable alternative, either to be, by observing the proprieties, only an elegant and useful writer, or to be, by respecting nothing, an author fascinating and deadly.

It is impossible that Voltaire should content you, and impossible that he should not please you.

Voltaire introduced and put in vogue such luxury in literary work, that one can no longer offer ordinary viands except on dishes of gold or silver. So much thought to please his reader gives evidence of more vanity than virtue, a stronger wish to fascinate than to serve, more ambition than authority, more art than nature; and all these attractions require rather a great master than a great man.

J. J. Rousseau had a voluptuous mind. In his writings the soul is blended with the body, and never leaves it. No man ever gave such an impression of flesh touching spirit and of the delights of their marriage.

Rousseau gave, if I may so speak, bowels to words, infused into them such a charm, savors so subtly sweet, energies so potent, that his writings affect the soul somewhat as do those forbidden pleasures that extinguish the taste and intoxicate the reason.

When we have read Buffon, we think ourselves learned. When we have read Rousseau, we think ourselves virtuous. But for all that we are neither the one nor the other.

From Rousseau, we learn to be discontented with every thing, except ourselves.

For thirty years Petrarch adored, not the person, but the image of Laura; so much easier is it to preserve one's sentiments and one's ideas than one's sensations. Thence came the fidelity of the ancient knights.

The *dic mihi, Musa* (say, O Muse!) is wanting to the tales of Boccaccio. He adds nothing to what was told him, and his inventions never go beyond the field formed by his memory. His narrative ends where ends the common story; he respects it as he would respect the truth.

Corneille is reproached with his grand words and his grand sentiments; but, in order to raise ourselves, and not to be soiled by the baseness of the earth, we need on all occasions stilts.

An irreligious piety, a corrupting severity, a dogmatism that destroys all authority: this is the character of Rousseau's philosophy.

The genius of Racine was in taste, like the ancients. His elegance is perfect, but it is not supreme, like that of Virgil.

No man knows better than Racine how to weave words, sentiments, thoughts, actions, events; and with him, events, actions, thoughts, sentiments, words, all are of silk.

The talent of Racine is in his works, but Racine himself is not in them. Hence he grew disgusted with them.

Boileau is a fine poet, but it is in the half-poetry.

Racine and Boileau are not springs of fresh water. A fine choice in imitation is their merit. It is their books that imitate books, and not their souls that imitate souls. Racine is the Virgil of the ignorant.

Moliere is calmly comic; he makes others laugh without laughing himself; that is what constitutes his excellence.

Alfieri is but a convict condemned by nature to the galleys of the Italian Parnassus.

In la Fontaine there is a plenitude of poetry which is found in no other French author.

Piron : a poet who played well on his Jew's-harp.

Literary sophistry is the art of varnishing thoughts with words. Words varnish thoughts when they make them shine, without adding to their beauty. There is a lustre necessary to a good style which is not precisely varnish; it is only cleanness. Style has sometimes a brilliancy like that of metals. Those who employ it do not varnish, properly speaking, but they gild what they say. One would think that they write with a more shining ink, or that, while their ink is still fresh on the paper, they have sprinkled it with powder from the wings of butterflies or with diamond-dust. All this goes neither to the soul nor the taste, but stops at the eyes of the mind, which, dazzled at first, grows at last tired of it. Esménard offers a perpetual example of this kind of artifice.

THE END.

LIST OF PUBLICATIONS

ISSUED AND FOR SALE BY

WILLIAM V. SPENCER,

203 WASHINGTON STREET, BOSTON.

☞ *The usual Discount to the Trade.* ☜

ANDERSON (I. H.) Patriotism at Home; or, The Young Invincibles. By the author of "Fred Freeland." With Four Illustrations, from original designs by CHAMPNEY. Printed on heavy paper, in handsome binding. 1 vol. 16mo. Price $1.50.

BERRY (MRS. M. E.) Celesta. A Girl's Book. 16mo. In press. $1.25.

——— Crooked and Straight. 16mo. In press. $1.25.

BRADLEE (MISS). Christus Victor. A Poem. Square 16mo. Flexible cloth. 50 cts.

——— Max Overman. 16mo. Paper. 50 cts.

——— Three Crowns. 16mo. Cloth. $1.25.

BULFINCH (REV. S. G., D.D.) Manual of the Evidences of Christianity. For Classes and Private Reading. 12mo. $1.25.

CALVERT (G. H.) Some of the Thoughts of JOSEPH JOUBERT. With a Biographical Notice. 16mo. Tinted paper. Cloth, bevelled. $1.50.

——— First Years in Europe. By the author of "Scenes and Thoughts in Europe," "The Gentleman," &c. 1 vol. 12mo. $1.75.

A finished and attractive narrative of a residence in Antwerp, Gottingen, Weimar, Edinburgh, and Paris, forty years ago; abounding in powerful criticisms of the religious and political sentiment of that time, exhibiting a close study of the literature and a familiar acquaintance with the literary men of that age.

CARPENTER (MISS MARY). Our Convicts. 2 vols. in 1. pp. 293 and 350. Octavo. $4.50.

CHANNING (MISS E. P.) The Adventures of a German Toy. A charming story for children, with three Illustrations. 75 cts.

COBBE (FRANCES POWER). Religious Duty. 12mo. Cloth, bevelled sides. $1.75.

―――― Studies New and Old, of Ethical and Social Subjects. Crown 8vo. Price $3.00.

CONTENTS: Christian Ethics and the Ethics of Christ; Self-Development and Self-Abnegation; The Sacred Books of the Zoroastrians; The Philosophy of the Poor Laws; The Rights of Man and the Claims of Brutes; The Morals of Literature; The Hierarchy of Art; Decemnovenarianism; Hades.

FERNALD (REV. W. M.) God in his Providence. 12mo. Cloth. $1.50.

―――― A View at the Foundations; or, First Causes of Character. 12mo. Cloth. $1.00.

GREY (HESTER). Kitty Barton. A simple Story for Children. With One Illustration. 32mo. 60 cts.

HOLLISTER (G. H.) Thomas à Becket. A Tragedy, and other Poems. 16mo. $1.75.

LINCOLNIANA. In one vol., small quarto. pp. viii. and 344. $6.00. (Only 250 copies printed.)

MARTINEAU (JAS.) Essays: Philosophical and Theological. Crown Octavo. Tinted paper. $2.50.

☞ Other volumes of the series in preparation.

MILL (JOHN STUART). Dissertations and Discussions. 3 vols. 12mo. Cloth. Per vol., $2.25.

―――― The Examination of the Philosophy of Sir William Hamilton. 2 vols. 12mo. Cloth. Per vol., $2.25.

―――― The Positive Philosophy of Auguste Comte. 1 vol. 12mo. Cloth. $1.25.

MUZZEY (REV. A. B.) The Blade and the Ear. Thoughts for a Young Man. 16mo. Red edges, bevelled sides, $1.50; plain, $1.25.

NAVILLE (ERNEST). The Heavenly Father: Lectures on Modern Atheism. By ERNEST NAVILLE, late Professor of Philosophy in the University of Geneva. Translated from the French, by HENRY DORNTON, M. A. Published in a handsome 16mo volume. $1.75.

"A thorough grappling with some of the most subtle and profound questions of the age. 'The Revival of Atheism,' &c. The author is thoroughly evangelical, and has treated his subjects with a masterly scholarship and ability. We hail all such books as the fulfilment of the Scripture promise, 'When the enemy shall come in like a flood, the spirit of the Lord shall lift up a standard against him.'"

REED (WM. HOWELL). Hospital Life in the Army of the Potomac. 16mo. $1.25.

STAHR (Adolf).   The Life and Works of Gotthold
Ephraim Lessing.   Translated from the German of Adolf
Stahr, by E. P. Evans, Ph. D., Michigan University. 2 vols.
Crown octavo. $5.00.

THURSTON (Mrs. Elizabeth A.) The Little Wrinkled
Old Man. A Christmas Extravaganza, and other Trifles. Illustrated. 75 cts.

TOWLE (Geo. M.) Glimpses of History. 1 vol. 16mo.
Bevelled boards. $1.50.

TOWNSEND (Miss Virginia F.) Darryll Gap; or,
Whether it Paid. A Novel. 1 vol. 12mo. pp. 456. $1.75.

A book of great force and power, dealing with the follies, the errors,
and the extravagance of this great sensational age. Depicting life
among those who have suddenly acquired wealth, and displaying lessons of devotion and self-sacrifice, drawn from a new field, hitherto
untrod by the novelist. The *Boston Transcript* says of it:—

"The story is thoroughly American in tone, scenery, incident, and
characters; it is to American life what Miss Bremer's 'Home' is to
life in Sweden. Like the Swedish tale, simple, natural in incident, its
characters have each a powerful individuality which takes hold at once
upon the interest and sympathies of the reader. The drama of the
story is artistic, and though its materials are drawn from the simple,
human, every-day life of our homes, the power of the book is felt to its
close; the moral lessons it unobtrusively teaches, cannot fail to sink
deep into the hearts of all who read it."

WARE (Rev. J. F. W.) Home Life: What it Is, and What
it Needs. 16mo. Cloth. Red edges, bevelled sides. $1.25.

⁎⁎* Copies of either of the above, or any book published in the United
States, sent by mail, free of postage, on receipt of price.